Sound Partners

Patricia Vadasy

Susan Wayne

Rollanda O'Connor

Joseph Jenkins

Kathleen Pool

Mary Firebaugh

Julia Peyton

A Tutoring

Program in

Phonics-Based

Early Reading

LESSONS

Sopris West®
EDUCATIONAL SERVICES

A Cambium Learning® Company

BOSTON, MA • LONGMONT, CO

Printed in the United States of America
Published and Distributed by

Sopris West®
EDUCATIONAL SERVICES

A Cambium Learning® Company

17855 Dallas Parkway, Suite 400 • Dallas, TX 75287
800-547-6747 • www.voyagersopris.com

Contents

apple

moon

a   a   m   a

m   m   a   a

a   a   m   a

a   m

Say the Sounds

▶ "Point to each letter. Say the sound."

▶ "The letter <u>a</u> is one of the vowels."

"Write the letter that makes the _____ sound."

Choose both sounds to practice.

First Sounds

▶ "What's the first sound in _____? Say the sound and point to that letter."

Use:

at	moon
man	mat
apple	monkey
actor	astronaut

Segmenting

▶ "Break this word into three parts."

mat	sat
pig	cap
dog	

Auditory exercise— use the segmented box as a visual cue.

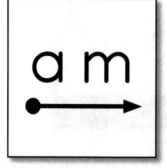

Word Reading

▶ "Point as you stretch out the sounds in the word."

"What sound does _____ **start** with?"

"What sound does _____ **end** with?"

"Now you spell _____."

Tutor Notes *Always have student repeat/say the word before spelling. Always have student read all words after spelling them.*

s S
sun

a   s   m   a

apple   moon

m   s   s   a

s   a   m   a

a   s   m

Say the Sounds

▶ "Point to each letter. Say the sound."

"Write the letter that makes the _____ sound."

Choose all three sounds.

First Sounds

▶ "What's the first sound in _____? Say the sound and point to that letter."

Use:

soup	apple
Sam	mat
sun	at
monkey	

Segmenting

▶ "Break this word into three parts."

mat	sat
Sam	moon
top	

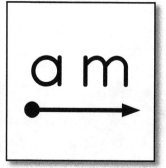

Word Reading

▶ "Point as you stretch out the sounds in the word."

"What sound does _____ **start** with?"

"What sound does _____ **end** with?"

"Now you spell _____."

If student has difficulty spelling, use the segmenting boxes to model:

▶ "How many sounds in _____?"

"What letter goes in the first box?"

Use the segmenting boxes.

t T
table

s	a	m	t
sun	apple	moon	

t	s	a	m

t	m	t	a

t	m	s	a

Say the Sounds

▶ "Point to each letter. Say the sound."

"Write the letter that makes the _____ sound."

Choose three or more sounds: include the newest sound, a difficult sound, and an easy sound.

First Sounds

▶ "What's the first sound in _____? Say the sound and point to that letter."

Use:

table	top
Sam	met
tiger	sun
sat	at
mud	apple

Segmenting

▶ "Break this word into three parts."

mat	can
pot	dog
man	

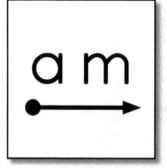

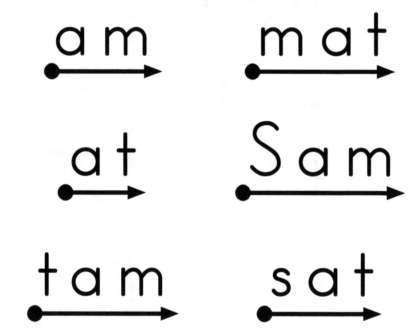

Word Reading

▶ "Point as you stretch out the sounds in the word."

"Now say it fast."

"What sound does _____ **start** with?"

"What sound does _____ **end** with?"

"Now you spell _____."

Choose three words for student to spell and read.

If student has difficulty spelling, use segmenting boxes to model.

▶ "Read this sentence. Point to each word."

Sam sat at <u>a</u> mat.

 Supply the sight word <u>a</u>.

tT
table

s	a	m	t
sun	apple	moon	

a	s	t	a
m	a	t	a
m	a	m	s

Say the Sounds

▶ "Point to each letter. Say the sound."

"Write the letter that makes the _____ sound."

Choose three or more sounds: include the newest sound, a difficult sound, and an easy sound.

Segmenting

▶ "Break this word into three parts."

moon	coat
sit	rake
sun	

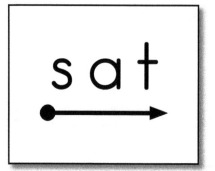

sat   mat

at   tam

am   Sam

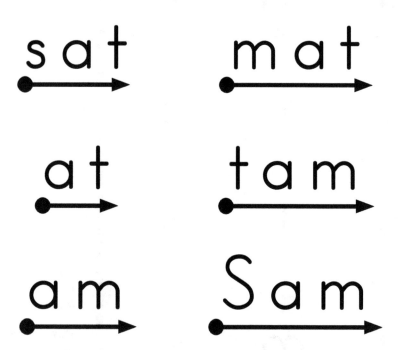

Sam sat at <u>a</u> mat.

Word Reading

▶ "Point as you stretch out the sounds in the word."

"Now say it fast."

"What sound does _____ **start** with?"

"What sound does _____ **end** with?"

"Now you spell _____."

Choose three words for student to spell and read.

▶ "Read this sentence. Point to each word."

 Supply the sight word <u>a</u>.

cC

cat

c   s   m   t

     sun   moon   table

a   c   t   s

apple

c   t   m   a

Say the Sounds

▶ "Point to each letter. Say the sound."

"Write the letter that makes the _____ sound."

Choose three or more sounds: include the newest sound, a difficult sound, and an easy sound.

Segmenting

▶ "Break this word into three parts."

mad	sock
cane	mug
ship	

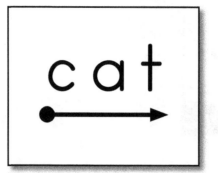

Word Reading

▶ "Point as you stretch out the sounds in the word."

"Now say it fast."

"What sound does _____ **start** with?"

"What sound does _____ **end** with?"

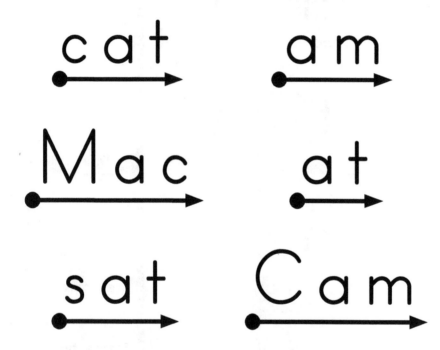

"Now you spell _____."

Choose three words for student to spell and read.

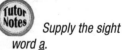 *Always have student repeat/say the word before spelling. Always have student read all words after spelling them.*

A cat sat at a mat.

▶ "Read this sentence. Point to each word."

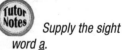 *Supply the sight word a.*

dD
dog

d   s   m   t

     sun   moon   table

m   a   c   d

     apple   cat

c   d   t   s

m   a   s   d

Say the Sounds

▶ "Point to each letter. Say the sound."

▶ "This sound /d/ is a lot like the /t/ sound. But your throat vibrates when you say /d/."

"Put your hand on your throat and say each sound:

/d/   /t/ "

"Write the letter that makes the _____ sound."

Segmenting

▶ "Break this word into three parts."

dog	Mac
kite	sad
time	

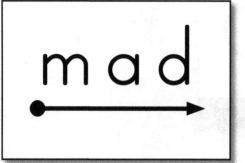

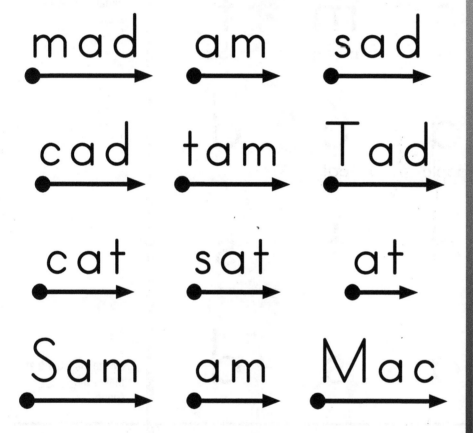

Sam <u>and</u> Mac sat.

<u>A</u> cat sat.

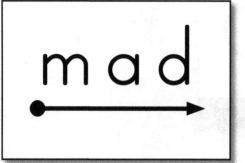

mad · am · sad

cad · tam · Tad

cat · sat · at

Sam · am · Mac

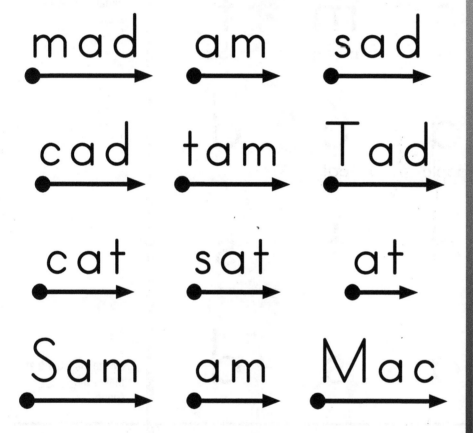

Sam <u>and</u> Mac sat.

<u>A</u> cat sat.

Lesson 6 cont'd

Word Reading

▶ "Point <u>as</u> you stretch out the sounds in the word."

"Now say it fast."

"What sound does _____ **start** with?"

"What sound does _____ **end** with?"

"Now you spell _____."

Choose three words for student to spell and read.

▶ "Read these sentences. Point to each word."

 *Supply the sight words <u>and</u> and <u>a</u>.*

NEW!
Book Reading

▶ Read *Mat*.

nN
nail

s   n   m   t
sun   moon table

n   a   c   d
     apple   cat   dog

c   a   n   m

Say the Sounds

▶ "Point to each letter. Say the sound."

▶ "This sound /n/ is a lot like the /m/ sound. When you say /m/, your lips close. When you say /n/, your lips stay open and you can feel your tongue touch the roof of your mouth."

"Say each sound:

    /n/   /m/ "

"Write the letter that makes the _____ sound."

Segmenting

▶ "Break this word into three parts."

Nat	sad
chip	rope
tap	

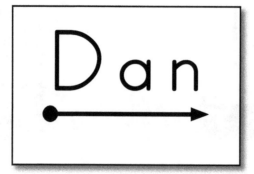

Dan

Dan   sad   Tad

am   ad   and

Sam   cad   mat

tan   Mac   sat

Sam <u>and</u> Tad sat at <u>a</u> mat.

▶ "Point as you stretch out the sounds in the word."

"Now say it fast."

"What sound does _____ **start** with?"

"What sound does _____ **end** with?"

"Now you spell _____."

Choose three words for student to spell and read.

▶ "Read this sentence. Point to each word."

 *Supply the sight words <u>a</u> and <u>and</u>.*

Book Reading

▶ Read *Mat.*

o O

octopus

o d n t

  dog nail table

m a o s

moon apple sun

o n c o

   cat

Say the Sounds

▶ "Point to each letter. Say the sound."

▶ "The letter o is one of the vowels."

"Write the letter that makes the _____ sound."

Segmenting

▶ "Break this word into three parts."

  moss pig
   sag tack
   wig

cot

cot Tom sad

cat sod Dot

mom not dad

nod on and

Mom nod<u>s</u> at Dot <u>and</u> at Tom.

▶ "Point as you stretch out the sounds in the word."

"Now say it fast."

"What sound does _____ **start** with?"

"What sound does _____ **end** with?"

"Now you spell _____."

Choose three words for student to spell and read.

▶ "Read this sentence. Point to each word."

Tutor Notes *Supply the word ending -s and the sight word and.*

Book Reading

▶ Read *Sam*.

o O
octopus

o	n	d	m
	nail	dog	moon
a	s	n	t
apple	sun		table
m	o	c	s
		cat	
t	c	m	d

"Write the letter that makes the _____ sound."

Segmenting

▶ "Break this word into three parts."

mad	sock
tape	dime
mom	

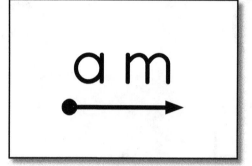

▶ "Point as you stretch out the sounds in the word."

"Now say it fast."

"What sound does _____ **start** with?"

"What sound does _____ **end** with?"

am   sad   Mac

Dot   mat   Tom

Mac   nod   con

cot   Dan   not

"Now you spell _____."

Choose three words for student to spell and read.

▶ "Read these sentences. Point to each word."

Mac <u>has</u> <u>a</u> cat.
Sad Tom <u>has</u> <u>no</u> cat.

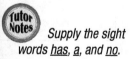 *Supply the sight words <u>has</u>, <u>a</u>, and <u>no</u>.*

Book Reading

▶ Read *Sam.*

hH
hat

a
apple

h

m
moon

t
table

n
nail

h

c
cat

m

o
octopus

a

d
dog

c

s
sun

h

o

d

Say the Sounds

▶ "Point to each letter. Say the sound."

"Write the letter that makes the _____ sound."

Segmenting

▶ "Break this word into three parts."

dot   pan

moss   hat

sad

hot

hot	Mac	dot
mad	and	cat
hat	cod	cot
not	ham	and
had	mat	at

Mac had <u>a</u> cat. Mac <u>and</u> cat sat on <u>a</u> cot.

Word Reading

▶ "Sound these out and say them fast."

"What sound does _____ **start** with?"

"What sound does _____ **end** with?"

"Now you spell _____."

Choose three words for student to spell and read.

Tutor Notes *Always have student repeat/say the word before spelling. Always have student read all words after spelling them.*

▶ "Read these sentences. Point to each word."

Tutor Notes *Supply the sight words <u>a</u> and <u>and</u>.*

Book Reading

▶ Read *Sam*.

Mastery Test 1

Use with Mastery Test 1—Tester Recording Sheet (see *Tutor Handbook*).

Sounds

▶ "Point to each letter. Say the sound."

h   m   a

s   t   n

d   o   c

(Provide student with Mastery Test 1—Student Recording Sheet found in *Tutor Handbook*.)

"Write the letter that makes the _____ sound."

Word Reading

▶ "Sound these words out, then read them fast."

mad   hot   cod

dot   cat   sad

and   ham   had

sat   Sam   Mac

(Provide student with Mastery Test 1—Student Recording Sheet found in *Tutor Handbook*.)

Spelling

"I say the word, and you write the word."

g G

girl

o	h	m	t
octopus	hat	moon	table
o	n	g	h
	nail		
g	a	d	c
	apple	dog	cat
s	g	o	d
sun			

Say the Sounds

▶ "Point to each letter. Say the sound."

"Write the letter that makes the _____ sound."

Segmenting

▶ "Break this word into three parts."

bake	Tad
dot	cat
sag	

got

got	tag	hat
Sam	and	on
nag	cog	not
mat	at	sad
sag	Mac	mom

Word Reading

▶ "Sound these out and say them fast."

"What sound does _____ **start** with?"

"What sound does _____ **end** with?"

"Now you spell _____."

Choose three words for student to spell and read.

Tutor Notes *Always have student repeat/say the word before spelling. Always have student read all words after spelling them.*

NEW!
Sight Words

► "Today we learn two sight words. We don't sound out sight words. Sight words are words we just have to remember."

► "This word is _____."

"You read it."

"Point and spell."

"What word?"

► "Read these sentences. Point to each word."

a

The

Sam sat on a cat!
The cat sat on a hat!

Book Reading

► Read *Sam*.

r R

rat

a
apple

g
girl

m
moon

t
table

r

n
nail

g

h
hat

o
octopus

r

d
dog

c
cat

s
sun

r

o

d

Say the Sounds

▶ "Point to each letter. Say the sound."

✎ "Write the letter that makes the _____ sound."

Segmenting

▶ "Break this word into three parts."

Sam	map
rag	hot
dog	

rat

rat	am	ran
mat	hog	tan
hat	tag	on
not	ham	rag
Nat	hot	cod

Word Reading

▶ "Sound these out and say them fast."

"What sound does _____ **start** with?"

"What sound does _____ **end** with?"

"Now you spell _____."

Choose three words for student to spell and read.

The   a

The man got mad at the cat. Sad cat.

Sight Words

▶ *Have student read, point and spell, and then reread each word.*

▶ "Read these sentences. Point to each word."

Book Reading

▶ Read *Dot*.

b B

ball

r	h	b	t
rat	hat		table
b	n	o	m
	nail	octopus	moon
d	a	g	c
dog	apple	girl	cat
s	r	o	b
sun			

Say the Sounds

▶ "Point to each letter. Say the sound."

🖉 "Write the letter that makes the _____ sound."

Segmenting

▶ "Break this word into three parts."

mat	hog
gate	rock
cat	

bat

bat   sob   bag

tag   Sam   nab

ban   and   not

cab   ham   mob

bog   sob   sad

Word Reading

▶ "Sound these out and say them fast."

"What sound does _____ **start** with?"

"What sound does _____ **end** with?"

"Now you spell _____."

Choose three words for student to spell and read.

in

The   a   in

Sight Words

▶ "This word is _____."

  "You read it."

  "Point and spell."

  "What word?"

▶ *Have student read, point and spell, and then reread each word.*

▶ "Read these sentences. Point to each word."

The man had a cat and a hog and a bat! The hog and the cat ran. The bat got in a hat.

Book Reading

▶ Read *Dot*.

b B
ball

a	r	b	t
apple	rat		table
g	n	c	h
girl	nail	cat	hat
o	b	t	m
octopus			moon
g	h	r	b

Say the Sounds

▶ "Point to each letter. Say the sound."

"Write the letter that makes the _____ sound."

Segmenting

▶ "Break this word into three parts."

rag	boat
time	hat
not	

bat

bat	nod	ban
hot	sob	ran
bag	rag	hat
bog	bad	tan
nab	rat	Mag

Word Reading

▶ "Sound these out and say them fast."

"What sound does _____ **start** with?"

"What sound does _____ **end** with?"

"Now you spell _____."

Choose three words for student to spell and read.

as   has

the   A

as   has   in

The man has a hat.
The dog got the hat.

▶ "This word is _____."

"You read it."

"Point and spell."

"What word?"

▶ *Have student read, point and spell, and then reread each word.*

▶ "Read these sentences. Point to each word."

Book Reading

▶Read *Mac.*

i I

itch

Say the Sounds

▶ "Point to each letter. Say the sound."

▶ "The letter i is one of the vowels."

a   r   b   i

apple   rat   ball

i   n   c   o

           nail   cat   octopus

m   b   g   c

moon   girl

i   h   s   b

           hat   sun

"Write the letter that makes the _____ sound."

Segmenting

▶ "Break this word into three parts."

Mit   hot
nap   bag
did

it

Word Reading

▶ "Sound these out and say them fast."

"What sound does _____ **start** with?"

"What sound does _____ **end** with?"

it	tin	dim
ban	dig	tab
in	rag	sod
sat	hit	bag
got	sit	bin

"Now you spell _____."

Choose three words for student to spell and read.

the   A

as   has

. . . .

▶ "Read these sentences. Point to each word."

A cat ran at the dog.
A man ran at the cat.
The cat got sad and
hid.

Book Reading

▶ Read *Mac*.

i I

itch

a	r	b	t
apple	rat	ball	table
g	n	c	i
girl	nail	cat	
o	b	r	n
octopus			
i	m	d	b
	moon	dog	

Say the Sounds

▶ "Point to each letter. Say the sound."

"Write the letter that makes the _____ sound."

Segmenting

▶ "Break this word into three parts."

dog	poke
hit	nail
cash	

in

in	bag	dig
hid	on	can
and	rid	dab
cot	tin	big
dim	had	rig

Word Reading

▶ "Sound these out and say them fast."

"What sound does _____ **start** with?"

"What sound does _____ **end** with?"

"Now you spell _____."

Choose three words for student to spell and read.

is	his

as	has	the
his	as	a
is	his	as
a	the	is

The cat is on his cot. Tim got the cat. The cat is sad.

▶ "This word is _____."

"You read it."

"Point and spell."

"What word?"

▶ *Have student read, point and spell, and then reread each word.*

▶ "Read these sentences. Point to each word."

Book Reading

▶ Read *Dot and the Dog*.

a   r   b   t

apple rat ball table

d   n   c   b

dog nail cat

o   m   n   s

octopus moon sun

g   h   r   i

girl hat itch

Say the Sounds

▶ "Point to each letter. Say the sound."

"Write the letter that makes the _____ sound."

Segmenting

▶ "Break this word into three parts."

sail ripe
nap miss
bake

got

got	sit	hot
Mit	not	hit
did	mat	rag
Mac	hid	dog
cat	bat	can

Word Reading

▶ "Sound these out and say them fast."

"What sound does _____ **start** with?"

"What sound does _____ **end** with?"

"Now you spell _____."

Choose three words for student to spell and read.

isn't

a	his	is
the	isn't	his
has	isn't	as

Tim has his cat in his hat. Isn't the cat hot in his hat?

Sight Words

▶ "This word is _____."

"You read it."

"Point and spell."

"What word?"

▶ "Isn't is a short way to say is not. This mark (') is called an apostrophe. We call these words contractions."

▶ *Have student read, point and spell, and then reread each word.*

▶ "Read these sentences. Point to each word."

Book Reading

▶ Read *Dot and the Dog*.

pP
pig

a	r	i	p
apple	rat	itch	
g	n	d	h
girl	nail	dog	hat
i	p	o	c
		octopus	cat
a	b	p	b
	ball		

Say the Sounds

▶ "Point to each letter. Say the sound."

"Write the letter that makes the _____ sound."

Segmenting

▶ "Break this word into three parts."

nap	Mit
sit	bog
pig	

pot

pot	hop	bop
pin	nap	rip
pig	mop	ram
pit	rap	dip
pan	bat	map

Word Reading

▶ "Sound these out and say them fast."

"What sound does _____ **start** with?"

"What sound does _____ **end** with?"

"Now you spell _____."

Choose three words for student to spell and read.

of

is   the   of

has   as   his

the   of   isn't

Tim has a bat. Is the bat in his bag? Isn't his bag on top of the tin can? His cat is in the bag!

Sight Words

▶ "This word is _____."

"You read it."

"Point and spell."

"What word?"

▶ *Have student read, point and spell, and then reread each word.*

▶ "Read these sentences. Point to each word."

Book Reading

▶ Read *Dot and Mit.*

w W

window

a	p	w	t
apple			table
	pig		
p	w	c	i
		cat	itch
w	b	o	c
	ball	octopus	
h	p	d	b
hat		dog	

"Write the letter that
makes the _____
sound."

Segmenting

▶ "Break this word into
three parts."

big	can
ran	wag
mop	

win

cap   wag   pat

bin   cot   wig

had   win   and

pad   Mac   wit

rag   hot   did

Word Reading

▶ "Sound these out and say them fast."

"What sound does _____ **start** with?"

"What sound does _____ **end** with?"

"Now you spell _____."

Choose three words for student to spell and read.

you

isn't   you   the

has   as   of

is   you   his

The man is big. His hat is big. A big cat can sit in his big hat.

▶ "This word is _____."

"You read it."

"Point and spell."

"What word?"

▶ *Have student read, point and spell, and then reread each word.*

▶ "Read these sentences. Point to each word."

Book Reading

▶ Read *Dot and Mit.*

j J

jet

m
moon

s
sun

b
ball

j

i
itch

p
pig

w
window

r
rat

g
girl

r

n
nail

a
apple

d
dog

j

i

w

Say the Sounds

▶ "Point to each letter. Say the sound."

"Write the letter that makes the _____ sound."

Segmenting

▶ "Break this word into three parts."

win	did
jam	ran
pig	

jog

hog	wig	did
bad	job	dad
jam	hit	jot
pad	Jim	got
cat	wag	jig

Word Reading

▶ "Sound these out and say them fast."

"What sound does _____ **start** with?"

"What sound does _____ **end** with?"

"Now you spell _____."

Choose three words for student to spell and read.

Tutor Notes *Always have student repeat/say the word before spelling. Always have student read all words after spelling.*

Sight Words

▶ "This word is _____."

"You read it."

"Point and spell."

"What word?"

▶ *Have student read, point and spell, and then reread each word.*

to

you	to	is
to	as	has
of	his	to
isn't	the	you

Jig ran to Mac, and Mac and Jig ran to Mat. Jig is hot!

Mastery Test 2

Use with Mastery Test 2—Tester Recording Sheet (see *Tutor Handbook*).

g   r   b

i   p   w

j   o   d

Sounds

▶ "Point to each letter. Say the sound."

(Provide student with Mastery Test 2—Student Recording Sheet found in *Tutor Handbook*.)

"Write the letter that makes the _____ sound."

---

jog   rat   big

tin   wag   hop

mop   dim   pad

win   hit   jam

Word Reading

▶ "Sound these words out, then read them fast."

(Provide student with Mastery Test 2—Student Recording Sheet found in *Tutor Handbook*.)

Spelling

"I say the word and you write the word."

---

you   is   the   of

his   to   has   as

Sight Word Reading

▶ "Read these words."

uU
up

u

h	d	a
hat	dog	apple

b	p	w	i
ball	pig	window	itch

u	r	n	j
	rat	nail	jet

d	j	i	u
dog			

Say the Sounds

▶ "Point to each letter. Say the sound."

▶ "The letter u is a vowel, like a, i, and o."

 "Write the letter that makes the _____ sound."

Segmenting

▶ "Break this word into three parts."

hid	dig
Mac	jog
rip	

up

up	cot	hug
dud	jut	rip
cup	pat	Jim
rib	pup	jug
bug	cut	bud

Word Reading

▶ "Sound these out and say them fast."

"What sound does _____ **start** with?"

"What sound does _____ **end** with?"

"Now you spell _____."

Choose three words for student to spell and read.

to   the   of

his   has   isn't

you   is   as

▶ *Have student read, point and spell, and then reread each word.*

Dictate three sight words for student to spell and read.

Mag can run. Mag can get the pig. Mag isn't as hot as the pig.

▶ *"Read these sentences. Point to each word."*

more →

S

▶ *Point to the s:*

"I'm going to say hat with this ending. Hats."

"When we see or hear the s at the end of hat, we know there is more than one hat."

"Your turn. Touch the s and say hat with this ending."

▶ *Repeat with:*

cup	rug
mat	pup

▶ "Now you read these words."

▶ "Notice how the s can make two different sounds at the end of a word: /s/ or /z/. What is the last sound in:
    caps?"
    bags?"

▶ "Both sounds are spelled with an s."

pot	pots	cap	caps
bag	bags	cat	cats
sit	sits	dot	dots

(See the Additional Supplementary Reading Scope and Sequence in the *Tutor Handbook* for additional titles.)

Book Reading

▶ Read *Jig and Mag*.

u U

up

h
hat

a
apple

d
dog

u

p
pig

w
window

u

i
itch

r
rat

u

n
nail

j
jet

u

j

i

d
dog

Say the Sounds

▶ "Point to each letter. Say the sound."

▶ "The letter u is a vowel, like a, i, and o."

"Write the letter that makes the _____ sound."

Segmenting

▶ "Break this word into three parts."

mud	rash
shut	bog
cone	

jug

rib   wit   hug

rub   not   rim

dip   got   jig

bun   bug   jam

pad   run   cup

Word Reading

▶ "Sound these out and say them fast."

"What sound does _____ **start** with?"

"What sound does _____ **end** with?"

"What is the **middle** sound in _____?"

"Now you spell _____."

Choose three words for student to spell and read.

▶ *Have student read, point and spell, and then reread each word.*

the   as   his

has   you   is

of   isn't   to

Dictate three sight words for student to spell and read.

▶ "Read these sentences. Point to each word."

Jim ran to hug the dog. The dog had a run. The dog isn't sad!

s

Word Endings

▶ *Point to the s:*

"I'm going to say <u>hat</u> with this ending. <u>Hats</u>."

"When we see or hear the <u>s</u> at the end of <u>hat</u>, we know there is more than one hat."

"Your turn. Touch the <u>s</u> and say <u>hat</u> with this ending."

▶ *Repeat with:*

dog	cap
pin	bird

jug	jugs	wig	wigs
mat	mats	nut	nuts
bit	bits	rip	rips

▶ "Now you read these words."

▶ "Notice how the <u>s</u> can make two different sounds at the end of a word: /s/ or /z/. What is the last sound in:
    pups?"
    rugs?"

▶ "Both sounds are spelled with an <u>s</u>."

(See the Additional Supplementary Reading Scope and Sequence in the *Tutor Handbook* for additional titles.)

Book Reading

▶ Read *Jig and Mag*.

fF

fish

f	s	b	u
	sun	ball	up
i	p	w	f
itch	pig	window	
u	r	n	j
	rat	nail	jet
w	j	f	u

Say the Sounds

▶ "Point to each letter. Say the sound."

"Write the letter that makes the _____ sound."

Segmenting

▶ "Break this word into three parts."

tug	fan
pig	run
rug	

fun

fun	wag	rid
fin	Ruff	sad
fig	fan	jog
fad	fat	dot
Muff	had	fit

Word Reading

▶ "Sound these out and say them fast."

▶ "Some words end in ff. It sounds like /f/ and the second f is silent."

"What sound does _____ **start** with?"

"What sound does _____ **end** with?"

"What is the **middle** sound in _____?"

"Now you spell _____."

Choose three words for student to spell and read.

for

or

the	to
or	for
is	to
for	or

▶ "This word is _____."

  "You read it."

  "Point and spell."

  "What word?"

▶ *Have student read, point and spell, and then reread each word.*

Dictate three sight words for student to spell and read.

Today is the fun race. You can run or jog to win. The sun is hot. Rod ran in a hat.

▶ "Read these sentences. Point to each word."

Word Endings

▶ *Point to the s:*

"I'm going to say hat with this ending. Hats."

"When we see or hear the s at the end of hat, we know there is more than one hat."

"Your turn. Touch the s and say hat with this ending."

▶ *Repeat with:*

bike   bag
shop   can

S			

▶ "Now you read these words."

▶ "Notice how the s can make two different sounds at the end of a word: /s/ or /z/. What is the last sound in:
tops?"
mugs?"

▶ "Both sounds are spelled with an s."

can	cans	pup	pups
wag	wags	nut	nuts
bud	buds	rib	ribs

(See the Additional Supplementary Reading Scope and Sequence in the *Tutor Handbook* for additional titles.)

Book Reading

▶ Read *Muff and Ruff.*

f
fish

s
sun

u
up

a
apple

i
itch

p
pig

w
window

r
rat

g
girl

u

f

t
table

f

j
jet

d
dog

u

Say the Sounds

▶ "Point to each letter. Say the sound."

"Write the letter that makes the _____ sound."

Segmenting

▶ "Break this word into three parts."

pup	fog
cup	cap
rig	

fat

fat	up	win
pan	rot	sat
win	huff	bin
fog	puff	bad
hid	pin	dad

Word Reading

▶ "Sound these out and
say them fast."

"What sound does
_____ **start** with?"

"What sound does
_____ **end** with?"

"What is the **middle**
sound in _____?"

"Now you spell
_____."

*Choose three words
for student to spell
and read.*

can't   didn't

for   you

of   has

didn't   is

to   can't

Mat didn't run in the fog. Mat can't win the run in the fog.

Sight Words

▶ "This word is _____."

"You read it."

"Point and spell."

"What word?"

▶ "Can't is a short way to say cannot. Didn't is a short way to say did not. This mark (') is called an apostrophe. We call these words contractions."

▶ *Have student read, point and spell, and then reread each word.*

✏ *Dictate three sight words for student to spell and read.*

▶ "Read these sentences. Point to each word."

Word Endings

▶ *Point to the s:*

"I'm going to say <u>hat</u> with this ending. <u>Hats</u>."

"When we see or hear the <u>s</u> at the end of <u>hat</u>, we know there is more than one hat."

"Your turn. Touch the <u>s</u> and say <u>hat</u> with this ending."

▶ *Repeat with:*

cup	mug
mat	plane

s

▶ "Now you read these words."

▶ "Notice how the <u>s</u> can make two different sounds at the end of a word: /s/ or /z/. What is the last sound in:
    dots?"
    bags?"

▶ "Both sounds are spelled with an <u>s</u>."

pot	pots	cap	caps
bag	bags	cat	cats
sit	sits	dot	dots

(See the Additional Supplementary Reading Scope and Sequence in the *Tutor Handbook* for additional titles.)

Book Reading

▶ Read *Muff and Ruff*.

e E

Ed

Say the Sounds

▶ "Point to each letter. Say the sound."

▶ "Letter _e_ is a vowel, like _a_, _i_, _o_, and _u_."

m	t	b	u
moon	table	ball	up

e	f	w	d
	fish	window	dog

n	e	f	a
nail			apple

e	j	u	e
	jet		

✎ "Write the letter that makes the _____ sound."

Segmenting

▶ "Break this word into three parts."

pot	hot
cap	wet
Ben	

men		

men	tug	pet
rug	wet	fan
dig	jig	jam
red	Mac	dad
pat	cut	fed

Word Reading

▶ "Sound these out and say them fast."

"What sound does _____ **start** with?"

"What sound does _____ **end** with?"

"What is the **middle/vowel** sound in _____?"

"Now you spell _____."

Choose three words for student to spell and read.

come	some

for

can't

his

you

some

come

didn't

is

Sight Words

▶ "This word is _____."

"You read it."

"Point and spell."

"What word?"

▶ *Have student read, point and spell, and then reread each word.*

Dictate three sight words for student to spell and read.

▶ "Read these sentences. Point to each word."

Mag can't run. Mag got a cut. Mag didn't run to you or Dad. Mag had a bad leg.

(See the Additional Supplementary Reading Scope and Sequence in the *Tutor Handbook* for additional titles.)

Book Reading

▶ Read *10 Cut Ups*.

Supplementary: Read *Fun in the Sun*.

eE

Ed

Say the Sounds

▶ "Point to each letter. Say the sound."

e	s	f	t
	sun	fish	table

d	p	e	u
dog	pig		up

e	r	f	c
	rat		cat

u	j	e	b
	jet		ball

"Write the letter that makes the _____ sound."

Segmenting

 *Model four-part segmenting to introduce.*

▶ "Break this word into four parts."

pots	caps
skate	stop
rags	

pet

pet	hen	jet
rip	jug	pit
sap	jig	fin
dug	wag	rub
wet	tip	nut

Word Reading

▶ "Sound these out and say them fast."

"What sound does _____ **start** with?"

"What sound does _____ **end** with?"

"What is the **middle** sound in _____?"

"Now you spell _____."

Choose three words for student to spell and read.

into

is   into   for

come   some   can't

didn't   into   isn't

Peg hops into bed for a nap. Peg naps for a bit and gets up for a jog.

▶ "Read these sentences. Point to each word."

(See the Additional Supplementary Reading Scope and Sequence in the *Tutor Handbook* for additional titles.)

Book Reading

▶ Read *10 Cut Ups.*

Supplementary:
Read *Fun in the Sun.*

thumb

th

e
Ed

b
ball

a
apple

i
itch

th

w
window

o
octopus

h
hat

r
rat

t
table

th

u
up

th

e

f
fish

Say the Sounds

▶ "Point to each letter or letter pair. Say the sound."

▶ "<u>Th</u> makes **one** sound. The tongue goes between the teeth."

▶ "<u>Th</u> can sound like /th/ like in <u>thumb</u> and /th/ like in <u>feather</u>. Say each word and notice how your throat vibrates when you say <u>feather</u> and how it doesn't vibrate when you say <u>thumb</u>."

"Write the letter or letter pair that makes the _____ sound."

Segmenting

▶ "Break this word into four parts."

spot	kites
nuts	crab
slip	

that

fed   thin   path

net   bib   wet

then   rut   hat

rug   did   bath

pen   get   dad

Word Reading

▶ "Sound these out and say them fast."

"What sound does _____ **start** with?"

"What sound does _____ **end** with?"

"What is the **middle** sound in _____?"

"Now you spell _____."

Choose three words for student to spell and read.

were

into   for   were

come   were   some

didn't   or   isn't

▶ "This word is _____."

"You read it."

"Point and spell."

"What word?"

▶ *Have student read, point and spell, and then reread each word.*

Dictate three sight words for student to spell and read.

▶ "Read these sentences. Point to each word."

Ted and Jed were sad. The dog Rags can't dig in the mud. Rags had a bath. Dad is mad at Rags.

(See the Additional Supplementary Reading Scope and Sequence in the *Tutor Handbook* for additional titles.)

Book Reading

▶ Read *Peg and Ted*.

Supplementary:
Read *Up Pup*.

kite

Say the Sounds

▶ "Point to each letter or letter pair. Say the sound."

e Ed	k	th thumb	f fish
k	p pig	u up	e
g girl	th	n nail	t table
n	j jet	k	a apple

"Write the letter or letter pair that makes the _____ sound."

spot	kites
jump	flag
dust	

Kim

this	kid	that
gum	fed	wet
Kip	bag	keg
jam	than	kit
kid	fad	dub

Word Reading

▶ "Sound these out and say them fast."

"What sound does _____ **start** with?"

"What sound does _____ **end** with?"

"What is the **middle** sound in _____?"

"Now you spell _____."

Choose three words for student to spell and read.

he	me	we	be

come	were	of
be	into	he
is	for	some
to	you	we
didn't	me	the

Sight Words

▶ "This word is _____."

"You read it."

"Point and spell."

"What word?"

▶ *Have student read, point and spell, and then reread each word.*

Dictate three sight words for student to spell and read.

······························

Ruff and Muff were in the bath. Dad got wet. Kit got wet. We had fun!

▶ "Read these sentences. Point to each word."

(See the Additional Supplementary Reading Scope and Sequence in the *Tutor Handbook* for additional titles.)

Book Reading

▶ Read *Peg and Ted*.

Supplementary:
Read *Up Pup*.

Ll

lion

Say the Sounds

▶ "Point to each letter or letter pair. Say the sound."

l	e	k	f
	Ed	kite	fish

i	l	w	r
itch		window	rat

g	k	l	th
girl			thumb

e	l	g	d
			dog

"Write the letter or letter pair that makes the _____ sound."

Segmenting

▶ "Break this word into four parts."

last	fast
flop	drip
spin	

lot

pan	lop	fat
let	log	fell
that	pill	dug
lid	can	thin
mill	wit	path

Word Reading

▶ "Sound these out and say them fast."

▶ "Some words end in <u>ll</u>. It sounds like /l/ and the second <u>l</u> is silent."

▶ "What sound does _____ **start** with?"

"What sound does _____ **end** with?"

"What is the **middle** sound in _____?"

"Now you spell _____."

Choose three words for student to spell and read.

said

he	you	come
were	isn't	be
said	for	we
to	into	some
is	me	said

▶ "This word is _____."

"You read it."

"Point and spell."

"What word?"

▶ *Have student read, point and spell, and then reread each word.*

Dictate three sight words for student to spell and read.

The man said, "Some big logs fell into the path at the log mill."

▶ "Read these sentences. Point to each word."

(See the Additional Supplementary Reading Scope and Sequence in the *Tutor Handbook* for additional titles.)

Book Reading

▶ Read *Lad and the Fat Cat.*

Supplementary: Read *Pip and Pog.*

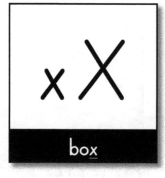

box

Say the Sounds

▶ "Point to each letter or letter pair. Say the sound."

▶ "The letter <u>x</u> makes **two** sounds, /k/ /s/."

x th e f

 thumb   Ed   fish

l p k x

lion   pig   kite

g u l o

girl   up   octopus

x j e d

jet   dog

"Write the letter or letter pair that makes the _____ sound."

Segmenting

▶ "Break this word into four parts."

drop   flap

mast   naps

step

box

box	this	fun
sat	kid	fox
six	set	wag
men	fix	wit
mix	that	nut

Word Reading

▶ "Sound these out and say them fast."

"What sound does _____ **start** with?"

"What sound(s) does _____ **end** with?"

"What is the **middle** sound in _____?"

Tutor Notes *Remember that* box *ends in* **two** *sounds.*

"Now you spell _____."

Choose three words for student to spell and read.

it's	let's

said	be	were
let's	it's	me
into	some	it's
you	is	let's
he	come	we

Kit said, "Let's pet the fox. It's in the pen." The man fed the fox a big hen.

(See the Additional Supplementary Reading Scope and Sequence in the *Tutor Handbook* for additional titles.)

Sight Words

▶ "This word is _____."

"You read it."

"Point and spell."

"What word?"

▶ "It's is a short way to say it is. Let's is a short way to say let us. This mark (') is called an apostrophe. We call these words contractions."

▶ *Have student read, point and spell, and then reread each word.*

Dictate three sight words for student to spell and read.

▶ "Read these sentences. Point to each word."

Book Reading

▶ Read *Lad and the Fat Cat.*

Supplementary: Read *Pip and Pog.*

Mastery Test 3

Use with Mastery Test 3—Tester Recording Sheet (see *Tutor Handbook*).

Sounds

▶ "Point to each letter or letter pair and say the sound."

u	f	e
th	k	l
x	i	b

"Write the letter(s) that makes the _____ sound."

(Provide student with Mastery Test 3—Student Recording Sheet found in *Tutor Handbook*.)

Word Reading

▶ "Sound these words out, then read them fast."

bud	fix	fed
let	bath	wet
path	red	box
kid	log	fun

Spelling

"I say the word, and you write the word."

(Provide student with Mastery Test 3—Student Recording Sheet found in *Tutor Handbook*.)

more →

said   for   can't   were

come   he   some   we

**Sight Word
Reading**

► "Read these words."

th	k	l	x
thumb	kite	lion	bo<u>x</u>

f	c	t	s
fish	cat	table	sun

l	x	e	a
		Ed	apple

x	o	i	u
	octopus	itch	up

fix

Muff	that	keg
bun	tug	gum
met	pit	nub
thin	Ned	bath
fox	lip	lot

► "Sound these out and say them fast."

"What sound does _____ **start** with?"

"What sound(s) does _____ **end** with?"

"What is the **middle** sound in _____?"

"Now you spell _____."

Choose three words for student to spell and read.

Tutor Notes *Always have student repeat/say the word before spelling. Always have student read all words after spelling them.*

was

come	he	said
to	some	were
was	into	we
of	me	was
you	it's	be

Mom said you were lost. Mom said that you fell into the pond. Were you lost? Did you get wet?

(See the Additional Supplementary Reading Scope and Sequence in the *Tutor Handbook* for additional titles.)

Sight Words

▶ "This word is _____."

"You read it."

"Point and spell."

"What word?"

▶ *Have student read, point and spell, and then reread each word.*

Dictate three sight words for student to spell and read.

▶ "Read these sentences. Point to each word."

Book Reading

▶ Read *Lad and the Fat Cat*.

vV

vet

Say the Sounds

▶ "Point to each letter or letter pair. Say the sound."

v	k	l	x
	kite	lion	bo<u>x</u>
j	b	h	v
jet	ball	hat	
th	x	e	a
thumb		Ed	apple
x	w	i	u
	window	itch	up

"Write the letter or letter pair that makes the _____ sound."

cats	flat
black	slip
dogs	

vet

vet	thin	mix
Kim	hen	van
path	lug	got
cup	vex	fed
vat	that	wet

Word Reading

▶ "Sound these out and say them fast."

"What sound does _____ **start** with?"

"What sound(s) does _____ **end** with?"

"What is the **middle** sound in _____?"

"Now you spell _____."

Choose three words for student to spell and read.

they

said	he	to
was	they	some
you	was	were
we	into	me
didn't	be	it's

They said, "Mag got into the vet's big van. The vet didn't let Mag sit in the cab."

(See the Additional Supplementary Reading Scope and Sequence in the *Tutor Handbook* for additional titles.)

Sight Words

▶ "This word is _____."

"You read it."

"Point and spell."

"What word?"

▶ *Have student read, point and spell, and then reread each word.*

Dictate three sight words for student to spell and read.

▶ "Read these sentences. Point to each word."

Book Reading

▶ Read *The Big Hat*.

yellow

Say the Sounds

▶ "Point to each letter or letter pair. Say the sound."

 th
thumb

 k
kite

l
lion

 x
bo<u>x</u>

y

 v
vet

t
table

s
sun

v

y

e
Ed

a
apple

n
nail

u
up

i
itch

y

🖊 "Write the letter or letter pair that makes the _____ sound."

Segmenting

▶ "Break this word into four parts."

hits   slope

skate   mist

step

yet

vat	yet	this
yap	yup	mix
yes	vet	red
bath	fit	nub
yen	van	yak

Word Reading

▶ "Sound these out and say them fast."

"What sound does _____ **start** with?"

"What sound(s) does _____ **end** with?"

"What is the **middle** sound in _____?"

"Now you spell _____."

Choose three words for student to spell and read.

I	I'm	I'll

they	me	were
was	into	I
come	were	be
said	I'll	I'm
was	you	some

Sight Words

▶ "This word is _____."

"You read it."

"Point and spell."

"What word?"

▶ "<u>I'm</u> is a short way to say <u>I am</u>. <u>I'll</u> is a short way to say <u>I will</u>. This mark (') is called an apostrophe. We call these words contractions."

▶ *Have student read, point and spell, and then reread each word.*

Dictate three sight words for student to spell and read.

They had a pet hen. I said, "I'll fix a pen for the pet hen. I'll fix a big pen for the red hen."

▶ "Read these sentences. Point to each word."

(See the Additional Supplementary Reading Scope and Sequence in the *Tutor Handbook* for additional titles.)

Book Reading

▶ Read *The Big Hat*.

zZ

zipper

th
thumb

z

l

x
box

z

y
yellow

l
lion

v
vet

r
rat

t
table

i
itch

e
Ed

s
sun

y

o
octopus

z

u
up

Say the Sounds

▶ "Point to each letter or letter pair. Say the sound."

✎ "Write the letter or letter pair that makes the _____ sound."

Segmenting

▶ "Break this word into four parts."

jump	blob
fist	frog
band	

zap

jazz	bet	fizz
zip	that	zig
leg	fax	bet
pup	zam	rig
fuzz	sip	thin

Word Reading

▶ "Sound these out and say them fast."

▶ "Some words end in zz. It sounds like /z/ and the second z is silent."

"What sound does _____ **start** with?"

"What sound(s) does _____ **end** with?"

"What is the **middle** sound in _____?"

"Now you spell _____."

Choose three words for student to spell and read.

all

I	some	all
was	they	come
said	he	was
I'll	all	it's
were	I'm	for

All of them said they didn't get to the top of the hill. It's a big hill. I'll get up on it yet!

(See the Additional Supplementary Reading Scope and Sequence in the *Tutor Handbook* for additional titles.)

Sight Words

▶ "This word is _____."

"You read it."

"Point and spell."

"What word?"

▶ *Have student read, point and spell, and then reread each word.*

Dictate three sight words for student to spell and read.

▶ "Read these sentences. Point to each word."

Book Reading

▶ Read *The Vet*.

sh Sh
sheep

Say the Sounds

▶ "Point to each letter or letter pair. Say the sound."

▶ "The pair <u>sh</u> makes **one** sound, /sh/."

sh	k	z	x
	kite	zipper	bo<u>x</u>

f	v	sh	y
fish	vet		yellow

z	p	e	d
	pig	Ed	dog

sh	o	i	u
	octopus	itch	up

"Write the letter or letter pair that makes the _____ sound."

Segmenting

▶ "Break this word into four parts."

last   rent

stick   ropes

land

fish

fish	shed	bun
rash	pig	that
fed	shop	cut
box	buzz	van
mash	band	vet
bus	lag	web

Word Reading

▶ "Sound these out and say them fast."

"What sound does _____ **start** with?"

"What sound does _____ **end** with?"

"What is the **middle/ vowel** sound in _____?"

"Now you spell _____."

Choose three words for student to spell and read.

come	all	I'm
he	you	said
I'll	they	were
some	all	was
isn't	was	into
I'll	we	they

▶ *Dictate three sight words for student to spell and read.*

All of the cats ran in the mud. They were all bad! Let's get them in the bath.

▶ "Read these sentences. Point to each word."

(See the Additional Supplementary Reading Scope and Sequence in the *Tutor Handbook* for additional titles.)

Book Reading

▶ Read *The Vet.*

sh Sh

sheep

sh   y   l   z
      yellow   lion   zipper

sh   c   t   s
      cat   table   sun

v   h   e   a
vet   hat   Ed   apple

z   o   w   u
     octopus   window   up

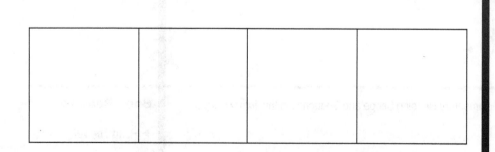

Say the Sounds

▶ "Point to each letter or letter pair. Say the sound."

"Write the letter or letter pair that makes the _____ sound."

Segmenting

▶ "Break this word into four parts."

most	cups
spill	slope
fist	

bash

bash   shot   sand

zap   fax   dish

shin   band   hand

fox   vat   lash

thin   land   fuzz

sip   math   mat

Word Reading

▶ "Sound these out and say them fast."

"What sound does _____ **start** with?"

"What sound(s) does _____ **end** with?"

"What is the **middle/ vowel** sound in _____?"

"Now you spell _____."

Choose three words for student to spell and read.

there

were	into	they
there	all	for
said	there	I
come	were	was
it's	they	there

Sight Words

▶ "This word is _____."

"You read it."

"Point and spell."

"What word?"

▶ *Have student read, point and spell, and then reread each word.*

Dictate three sight words for student to spell and read.

....

There were beds for all the cats—Fuzz, Nell, and Miss. They said, "This is the best."

▶ "Read these sentences. Point to each word."

(See the Additional Supplementary Reading Scope and Sequence in the *Tutor Handbook* for additional titles.)

Book Reading

▶ Read *Bow-Wow*.

ch Ch

cherry

Say the Sounds

▶ "Point to each letter or letter pair. Say the sound."

▶ "The letter pair <u>ch</u> makes **one** sound, /ch/."

ch

v
vet

y
yellow

x
bo<u>x</u>

z
zipper

j
jet

ch

b
ball

sh
sheep

x

h
hat

sh

ch

o
octopus

i
itch

u
up

"Write the letter or letter pair that makes the _____ sound."

Segmenting

▶ "Break this word into four parts."

mist	pots
flip	brake
flock	sent

chip

chip	fish	bent
rich	kid	chat
land	sent	that
sand	chop	such
tent	chin	rash

Word Reading

▶ "Sound these out and say them fast."

"What sound does _____ **start** with?"

"What sound(s) does _____ **end** with?"

"What is the **middle/vowel** sound in _____?"

"Now you spell _____."

Choose three words for student to spell and read.

you'll

were	there	they
you'll	all	were
said	you'll	there
into	I'm	we
all	there	they

▶ "This word is _____."

"You read it."

"Point and spell."

"What word?"

▶ *Have student read, point and spell, and then reread each word.*

Dictate three sight words for student to spell and read.

There is a big box on the step. Mom said that it isn't for us. She said that it is for Dad.

▶ "Read these sentences. Point to each word."

(See the Additional Supplementary Reading Scope and Sequence in the *Tutor Handbook* for additional titles.)

Book Reading

▶ Read *Bow-Wow*.

ch Ch
cherry

ch

y
yellow

l
lion

sh
sheep

h
hat

j
jet

t
table

ch

l

sh

e
Ed

z
zipper

ch

n
nail

i
itch

u
up

j

l

sh

y

Say the Sounds

▶ "Point to each letter or letter pair. Say the sound."

"Write the letter or letter pair that makes the _____ sound."

chin

chin   chop   rash

rich   fish   chip

chat   yet   sham

dash   box   kit

such   shut   wish

Word Reading

▶ "Sound these out and say them fast."

"What sound does _____ **start** with?"

"What sound(s) does _____ **end** with?"

"What is the **middle/ vowel** sound in _____?"

"Now you spell _____."

Choose three words for student to spell and read.

what

what's

all	I	what
into	they	there
all	let's	what's
said	were	was
they	I'll	all

"What a big red van! What's it for? They can't run it in the mud."

(See the Additional Supplementary Reading Scope and Sequence in the *Tutor Handbook* for additional titles.)

▶ "This word is _____."

   "You read it."

   "Point and spell."

   "What word?"

▶ "<u>What's</u> is a short way to say <u>what is</u>. This mark (') is called an apostrophe. We call these words contractions."

▶ *Have student read, point and spell, and then reread each word.*

Dictate three sight words for student to spell and read.

▶ "Read these sentences. Point to each word."

Book Reading

▶ Read *Ten Men*.

Supplementary: Read *Go Bus*.

Say the Sounds

▶ "Point to each letter or letter pair. Say the sound."

sh	ch	z	x
sheep	cherry	zipper	bo<u>x</u>

r	g	l	v
rat	girl	lion	vet

ch	y	e	a
	yellow	Ed	apple

sh	o	i	u
	octopus	itch	up

y	v	z	e
		zipper	

i	l	ch	sh

"Write the letter or letter pair that makes the _____ sound."

nut

nut	jet	best
nest	stop	flip
blob	west	chop
slum	ship	flag
chip	zip	clip

Word Reading

▶ "Sound these out and say them fast."

"What sound does _____ **start** with?"

"What sound(s) does _____ **end** with?"

"What is the **middle/ vowel** sound in _____?"

▶ "Bl, fl, cl, and sl are made up of **two** sounds."

"Now you spell _____."

Choose three words for student to spell and read.

said   they   all

there   for   what

they   you'll   there

was   I'm   what's

Sight Words

▶ *Have student read, point and spell, and then reread each word.*

Dictate three sight words for student to spell and read.

I didn't ask for fish and chips. Pat and Kit had chips and pop. They said that the chips were the best.

▶ "Read these sentences. Point to each word."

NEW!
Inside-Sound
Spelling Practice

"Listen to each word in this pair. One word has an inside sound that is hard to hear. Now spell the words."

sap	slap
hut	hunt
pump	pup
went	wet
sad	sand
lit	lint

(See the Additional Supplementary Reading Scope and Sequence in the *Tutor Handbook* for additional titles.)

Book Reading

▶ Read *Ten Men.*

Supplementary:
Read *Go Bus.*

wh Wh
whale

Say the Sounds

▶ "Point to each letter or letter pair. Say the sound."

▶ "The letter pair <u>wh</u> makes **one** sound, /wh/."

th
thumb

k
kite

wh

x
bo<u>x</u>

ch
cherry

wh

n
nail

l
lion

t
table

z
zipper

d
dog

ch

wh

e
Ed

y
yellow

i
itch

ch

th

t

e

🖊 "Write the letter or letter pair that makes the _____ sound."

whip

whip   ship   dish

chat   hush   wham

lot   whim   yet

vat   such   shut

when   chip   buzz

Word Reading

▶ "Sound these out and say them fast."

"What sound does _____ **start** with?"

"What sound(s) does _____ **end** with?"

"What is the **middle/ vowel** sound in _____?"

"Now you spell _____."

Choose three words for student to spell and read.

saw

what	saw	were
come	they	said
some	what	saw
there	they	said

▶ "This word is _____."

"You read it."

"Point and spell."

"What word?"

▶ *Have student read, point and spell, and then reread each word.*

Dictate three sight words for student to spell and read.

▶ "Read these sentences. Point to each word."

Come get some sand to dig. I can fill the dish with wet sand. I'll fill it and mash it.

Inside-Sound Spelling Practice

"Listen to each word in this pair. One word has an inside sound that is hard to hear. Now spell the words."

bent	bet
fan	flan
chimp	chip
plot	pot
hand	had
clamp	clap

(See the Additional Supplementary Reading Scope and Sequence in the *Tutor Handbook* for additional titles.)

Book Reading

▶ Read *The Red Hen*.

Mastery Test 4

Use with Mastery Test 4—Tester Recording Sheet (see *Tutor Handbook*).

Sounds

▶ "Point to each letter or letter pair and say the sound."

v	y	z
sh	ch	wh
e	th	u

(Provide student with Mastery Test 4—Student Recording Sheet found in *Tutor Handbook*.)

✎ "Write the letter(s) that makes the _____ sound."

Word Reading

▶ "Sound these words out, then read them fast."

fix	vex	yap
chop	yes	bash
zip	dish	whip
vet	rich	yet
such	wham	shop

(Provide student with Mastery Test 4—Student Recording Sheet found in *Tutor Handbook*.)

Spelling

✎ "I say the word, and you write the word."

they   I'll   what   saw

there   was   I'm   all

you'll   I   what's

wh Wh
whale

z	wh	l	sh
zipper		lion	sheep
ch	c	wh	y
cherry	cat		yellow
r	g	l	a
rat	girl		apple
wh	o	i	ch
	octopus	itch	
sh	r	c	ch

Say the Sounds

▶ "Point to each letter or letter pair. Say the sound."

"Write the letter or letter pair that makes the _____ sound."

when

when	shell	gosh
chin	much	with
rent	such	plug
chap	path	stag
whip	mush	plan

Word Reading

▶ "Sound these out and say them fast."

"What sound does _____ **start** with?"

"What sound(s) does _____ **end** with?"

"What is the **middle/vowel** sound in _____?"

"Now you spell _____."

Choose three words for student to spell and read.

Sight Words

▶ "This word is _____."

"You read it."

"Point and spell."

"What word?"

▶ *Have student read, point and spell, and then reread each word.*

Dictate three sight words for student to spell and read.

▶ "Read these sentences. Point to each word."

over

saw   there   all

over   they   were

saw   all   over

you'll   what   was

What is over there in the tent with the dog? It's a big log, isn't it? I saw the dog drag it in the tent.

Inside-Sound Spelling Practice

"Listen to each word in this pair. One word has an inside sound that is hard to hear. Now spell the words."

hand	had
rap	ramp
set	sent
limp	lip
lot	lost
best	bet

(See the Additional Supplementary Reading Scope and Sequence in the *Tutor Handbook* for additional titles.)

Book Reading

▶ Read *Sox the Fox.*

Say the Sounds

▶ "Point to each letter or letter pair. Say the sound."

x	wh	v	sh
bo<u>x</u>	whale	vet	sheep

ch	c	wh	p
cherry	cat		pig

u	d	l	e
up	dog	lion	Ed

wh	o	i	ch
	octopus	itch	

y	u	w	v
yellow		window	

l	i	e	u

"Write the letter or letter pair that makes the _____ sound."

when

when	stub	hush
bath	such	shed
chap	step	shod
much	chin	lump
pump	shim	wax

▶ "Sound these out and say them fast."

"What sound does _____ **start** with?"

"What sound(s) does _____ **end** with?"

"What is the **middle/ vowel** sound in _____?"

"Now you spell _____."

Choose three words for student to spell and read.

over   saw   were

into   what   they

saw   there   you'll

was   were   over

▶ *Have student read, point and spell, and then reread each word.*

Dictate three sight words for student to spell and read.

▶ "Read these sentences. Point to each word."

All of the fish were hot in the sun. They all swam over there. Some hid in the mud. Some hid in the sand.

Inside-Sound Spelling Practice

"Listen to each word in this pair. One word has an inside sound that is hard to hear. Now spell the words."

cap	camp
pest	pet
cap	clap
limp	lip
pop	plop
had	hand

Word Endings

▶ *Point to the <u>ed</u>:*

▶ "When we add <u>ed</u> to the end of a word, it means that something already happened."

▶ "I'm going to say <u>flip</u> with this ending. <u>Flipped</u>."

▶ "Your turn. Touch the <u>ed</u> and say <u>flip</u> with this ending."

▶ *Repeat with:*

hop	miss
rake	jump

ed

▶ "The <u>ed</u> ending has three different sounds, but they are all spelled <u>ed</u>. In these words the <u>ed</u> sounds like /t/."

▶ "Now you read these words."

skip	skipped	hum	hummed
pass	passed	slip	slipped
puff	puffed	limp	limped

(See the Additional Supplementary Reading Scope and Sequence in the *Tutor Handbook* for additional titles.)

Book Reading

▶ Read *Kittens*.

Supplementary:
Read *The Sad Cat*.

qu Qu
queen

Say the Sounds

▶ "Provide the cue word for letter pairs."

▶ "Point to each letter or letter pair. Say the sound."

▶ "Qu makes **two** sounds, /k/ /w/."

▶ "Sl, sk, and fl are each made up of **two** sounds."

x
box

wh
whale

l
lion

qu

ch
cherry

sl
slide

qu

y
yellow

qu

g
girl

sk
skunk

fl
flower

wh

f
fish

th
thumb

b
ball

g

qu

p
pig

b

"Write the letter or letter pair that makes the _____ sound(s)."

Provide the cue word for letter pairs.

quit		

quit	when	thin
pumped	flash	quilt
slash	quiz	whip
chipped	then	skims
flip	with	task

Word Reading

▶ "Sound these out and say them fast."

"What sound does _____ **start** with?"

"What sound(s) does _____ **end** with?"

"What is the **middle/ vowel** sound in _____?"

"Now you spell _____."

Choose three words for student to spell and read.

she	she's

over	saw	she
there	they	what
saw	were	she's
there	over	was
were	she	they

She saw the fish. She saw that there were lots of them. They were over there in the mud.

Sight Words

▶ "This word is _____."

"You read it."

"Point and spell."

"What word?"

▶ "She's is a short way to say she is. This mark (') is called an apostrophe. We call these words contractions."

▶ *Have student read, point and spell, and then reread each word.*

Dictate three sight words for student to spell and read.

▶ "Read these sentences. Point to each word."

ed

Word Endings

▶ *Point to the ed:*

▶ "When we add ed to the end of a word, it means that something already happened."

▶ "The ed ending in some words has the /d/ sound."

▶ "I'm going to say pull with this ending. Pulled."

▶ "Your turn. Touch the ed and say pull with this ending."

▶ *Repeat with:*

hum	fill
wag	tug

▶ "Now you read these words."

smell   smelled   pin   pinned

tug   tugged   jog   jogged

hum   hummed   spill   spilled

had   ha<u>n</u>d   hut   hu<u>n</u>t

lad   la<u>n</u>d   wet   we<u>n</u>t

lip   li<u>m</u>p   cap   ca<u>m</u>p

NEW!
Final <u>m</u> and <u>n</u> Blends

▶ "Today we start reading and spelling words with a final blend: two consonants that come after the vowel."

▶ "It can be very hard to hear both of these last letters. You must listen closely to hear the next to last letter. Say each pair with me. Listen closely for the underlined sound."

"Now spell these words. Notice whether the word ends in an <u>m</u> or <u>n</u> blend."

vet	went
hunt	lap
damp	vent

NEW!
Pair Practice

▶ "Let's do extra practice with our new letter pairs."

🖊 *Tutor dictate:* "Write the letters that make these sounds."

th	qu	fl
wh	sl	sk

▶ "Now read these words."

quit   skim   flat

slam   chug   moth

🖊 "Now spell these words."

flab	slug	skip
when	shop	chin

▶ "Now read these nonwords. These are made up words."

skup   shem   flig

wheb   slan   thip

🖊 "Now spell these nonwords."

sluz   skap   flet

(See the Additional Supplementary Reading Scope and Sequence in the *Tutor Handbook* for additional titles.)

Book Reading

▶ Read *Kittens.*

Supplementary:
Read *The Sad Cat.*

Say the Sounds

▶ "Point to each letter or letter pair. Say the sound."

qu
queen

wh
whale

v
vet

sh
sheep

fl
flower

f
fish

e
Ed

qu

sk
skunk

th
thumb

sl
slide

a
apple

sl

qu

i
itch

ch
cherry

v

w
window

y
yellow

wh

sl

sh

sk

ch

"Write the letter or letter pair that makes the _____ sound(s)."

Provide the cue word for letter pairs.

quiz

quiz	whip	much
skid	with	quit
when	bath	chaps
such	skips	thud
them	chimp	quilt

Word Reading

▶ "Sound these out and say them fast."

"What sound does _____ **start** with?"

"What sound(s) does _____ **end** with?"

"What is the **middle/ vowel** sound in _____?"

"Now you spell _____."

Choose three words for student to spell and read.

she   over   were

they   she's   saw

were   saw   into

there   they   I'll

▶ *Have student read, point and spell, and then reread each word.*

Dictate three sight words for student to spell and read.

The class had a quiz. Meg was ill. She missed the quiz.

▶ "Read these sentences. Point to each word."

ed

Lesson 44 cont'd

Word Endings

▶ *Point to the ed:*

▶ "When we add ed to the end of a word, it means that something already happened."

▶ "The ed ending in some words has the /ed/ sound. These words have an added syllable or beat when they end in ed."

▶ "I'm going to say pat with this ending. Patted."

▶ "Your turn. Touch the box and say pat with this ending."

▶ *Repeat with:*

    hunt   pet

▶ "Now you read these words."

mend   mended   rent   rented

test   tested   pet   petted

pat   patted   lift   lifted

Final <u>m</u> and <u>n</u> Blends

"I'll say these word pairs. First say each word and listen to hear if there is a /m/ or /n/ sound at the end of the word. Then spell the word pairs."

vet	vent
shut	shunt
lap	lamp
runt	rut
limp	lip

▶ "Now you read these words."

bet   bent   hung   hug

rap   ramp   had   hand

quip   skim   flat

chip   slap   whip

▶ "Now read these words."

"Now spell these words."

fled	thin	shed
skip	sled	when

chog   slup   flep

thet   skeb   cham

▶ "Now read these nonwords."

"Now spell these nonwords."

slep   quag   skib

(See the Additional Supplementary Reading Scope and Sequence in the *Tutor Handbook* for additional titles.)

Book Reading

▶ Read *Rub a Dub*.

Supplementary:
   Read *OK Kids*.

er

fern

Say the Sounds

▶ "Point to each letter or letter pair. Say the sound."

▶ "The letter pair <u>er</u> makes **one** sound, /er/."

z zipper	wh whale	l lion	er
ch cherry	er	wh	y yellow
qu queen	j jet	b ball	a apple
h hat	o octopus	er	sk skunk
u up	y	wh	qu

"Write the letter or letter pair that makes the _____ sound(s)."

Provide the cue word for letter pairs.

her

her	faster	fern
skips	letter	chill
when	Bert	helper
stern	hunter	quiz
crunched	bumper	robin

Word Reading

▶ "Sound these out and say them fast."

"What sound does _____ **start** with?"

"What sound(s) does _____ **end** with?"

"What is the **middle/vowel** sound in _____?"

"Now you spell _____."

Choose three words for student to spell and read.

saw	all	you'll
she	there	were
what	they	there
saw	she's	over

► *Have student read, point and spell, and then reread each word.*

Dictate three sight words for student to spell and read.

Was that you over there? Were they with you? Didn't they come with you?

► "Read these sentences. Point to each word."

ed

▶ *Point to the ed:*

▶ "When we add ed to the end of a word, it means that something already happened."

▶ "I'm going to say plan with this ending. Planned."

▶ "Your turn. Touch the box and say plan with this ending."

▶ *Repeat with:*

    bump   rent

▶ "Remember that ed has three sounds: /t/, /d/, and /ed/."

▶ "What sound does the ed make at the end of:

    mashed?"

    slugged?"

    chatted?"

▶ "Now you read these words."

drop	dropped	chat	chatted
plan	planned	mash	mashed
clap	clapped	slug	slugged

Final <u>m</u> and <u>n</u> Blends

"I'll say these word pairs. First say each word and listen to hear if there is a /m/ or /n/ sound at the end of the word. Then spell the word pairs."

pond	pod
hit	hint
chimp	chip
pup	pump
land	lad

▶ "Now you read these words."

lint   lit   sad   sand

hut   hunt   chant   chat

fern whip sled

skit flub that

▶ "Now read these words."

"Now spell these words."

when	pert	thud
term	fled	skim

fler quod skeb

thim slad chert

▶ "Now read these nonwords."

"Now spell these nonwords."

sker	shap	slem

(See the Additional Supplementary Reading Scope and Sequence in the *Tutor Handbook* for additional titles.)

Book Reading

▶ Read *Rub a Dub*.

Supplementary:
  Read *OK Kids*.

sw

swim

er   wh   sl   sh

       whale   slide   sheep

ch   u   er   sk

cherry   up   skunk

n   w   h   fl

nail   window   hat   flower

er   qu   i   sw

            itch

      queen

sl   sh   sw   sk

Say the Sounds

▶ "Point to each letter or letter pair. Say the sound."

▶ "Sw makes **two** sounds."

"Write the letter or letter pair that makes the _____ sound(s)."

Provide the cue word for letter pairs.

fern

fern	mask	step
slipper	her	whiz
swims	flash	herder
slump	stands	ask
skims	flip	swish

Word Reading

▶ "Sound these out and say them fast."

"What sound does _____ **start** with?"

"What sound(s) does _____ **end** with?"

"What is the **middle/ vowel** sound in _____?"

"Now you spell _____."

Choose three words for student to spell and read.

want

she	I'm	want
over	there	she
saw	they	want
what	all	there

She wants to run over there to be with her pet cat. Her cat is soft and licks her hand.

▶ "This word is _____."

"You read it."

"Point and spell."

"What word?"

▶ *Have student read, point and spell, and then reread each word.*

Dictate three sight words for student to spell and read.

▶ "Read these sentences. Point to each word."

Tutor Notes *Always supply underlined items.*

vowels: a, e, i, o, u

m<u>a</u>te	m<u>a</u>t	d<u>i</u>me	d<u>i</u>m
c<u>a</u>m	c<u>a</u>me	s<u>a</u>me	S<u>a</u>m
pl<u>a</u>n	pl<u>a</u>ne	h<u>a</u>te	h<u>a</u>t

NEW! Magic -e-

► "Here is the rule: If a word has an <u>e</u> at the end, the middle vowel says its name and the <u>e</u> is quiet. Let's practice this rule."

► *Point to each word and say:*

"Is there an <u>e</u> at the end of this word? Will the middle vowel say its name or its sound?"

"Let's sound out the word."

---

y

Word Endings

► *Point to the y:*

"I'm going to say <u>bump</u> with this ending. <u>Bumpy</u>."

"Your turn. Touch the <u>y</u> and say <u>bump</u> with this ending."

► *Repeat with:*

salt	sun
bump	snap

► "Now you read these words."

sun	sunny	Tim	Timmy
bug	buggy	flash	flashy
Dan	Danny	Till	Tilly

Final <u>m</u> and <u>n</u> Blends

"I'll say these word pairs. First say each word and listen to hear if there is a /m/ or /n/ sound at the end of the word. Then spell the word pairs."

sent	set
Ted	tend
chat	chant
clamp	clap
lend	led

▶ "Now you read these words."

slat   slant   chip   chimp

skimp   skip   bet   bent

▶ "Let's do extra practice with our new letter pairs."

Tutor dictate: "Write the letters that make these sounds."

er	sk	sl
qu	fl	sw

---

flap	slop	swim
chap	whip	shed

▶ "Now read these words."

"Now spell these words."

term	quip	when
swam	chug	verb

---

fler	skub	slev
cheg	nert	slaf

▶ "Now read these nonwords."

"Now spell these nonwords."

trag	sler	flob

(See the Additional Supplementary Reading Scope and Sequence in the *Tutor Handbook* for additional titles.)

Book Reading

▶ Read *Bump.*

Supplementary:
Read *0 to 10.*

tree

Say the Sounds

▶ "Point to each letter or letter pair. Say the sound."

▶ "<u>Ee</u> is our new vowel team. The two vowels together make **one** sound, /ee/."

▶ "<u>St</u> makes **two** sounds."

z
zipper

ee

l
lion

x
bo<u>x</u>

ch
cherry

qu
queen

ee

st
stop

r
rat

g
girl

p
pig

er
fern

sw
swim

ee

i
itch

sw

st

sk
skunk

ee

er

"Write the letter or letter pair that makes the _____ sound(s)."

Sound Partners

Lessons 155

stone

sheen	sweeps	sleep
went	glee	faster
steep	lifted	feed
cheeks	feel	whiz
steel	need	swish

Word Reading

▶ "Sound these out and say them fast."

"What sound does _____ **start** with?"

"What sound(s) does _____ **end** with?"

"What is the **middle/vowel** sound in _____?"

"Now you spell _____."

Choose three words for student to spell and read.

my	by

saw	she	by
want	my	over
what	there	by
they	it's	my

All my pets were over there by my dad. They went to sleep by his feet.

▶ "This word is _____."

"You read it."

"Point and spell."

"What word?"

▶ *Have student read, point and spell, and then reread each word.*

Dictate four sight words for student to spell and read.

▶ "Read these sentences. Point to each word."

vowels: a, e, i, o, u

m<u>o</u>p	m<u>o</u>pe	r<u>i</u>p	r<u>i</u>pe
t<u>a</u>p	t<u>a</u>pe	c<u>u</u>t	c<u>u</u>te
J<u>a</u>n	J<u>a</u>ne	t<u>u</u>b	t<u>u</u>be

▶ "Here is the rule: If a word has an <u>e</u> at the end, the middle vowel says its name and the <u>e</u> is quiet. Let's practice this rule."

▶ "Is there an <u>e</u> at the end of this word? Will the middle vowel say its name or its sound?"

▶ "Let's sound out the word."

▶ "The magic -e- can make the <u>u</u> say /oo/ or /y/ /oo/. Sometimes you have to try both to see which fits."

▶ *Point to the <u>y</u>:*

"I'm going to say <u>bump</u> with this ending. <u>Bumpy</u>."

"Your turn. Touch the <u>y</u> and say <u>bump</u> with this ending."

▶ *Repeat with:*

sleep	mud
fun	fish

▶ "Now you read these words."

weed	weedy	Bill	Billy
mush	mushy	skin	skinny
boss	bossy	Jim	Jimmy

| flee | stab | test |
| steep | stern | past |

▶ "Now read these words."

"Now spell these words."

| glee | stub | best |
| fleet | fern | mast |

| swee | stev | chee |
| fler | stap | dest |

▶ "Now read these nonwords."

"Now spell these nonwords."

| fleep | sterm | sheeb |

(See the Additional Supplementary Reading Scope and Sequence in the *Tutor Handbook* for additional titles.)

Book Reading

▶ Read *Bump*.

Supplementary:
Read *0 to 10*.

ee

tree

ck

truck

Say the Sounds

▶ "Point to each letter or letter pair. Say the sound."

▶ "Ck makes the last sound in truck. Ck comes only at the end of a word."

qu

queen

ee

st

stop

ck

ch

cherry

p

pig

wh

whale

er

fern

e

Ed

sw

swim

h

hat

ck

sl

slide

o

octopus

d

dog

ee

sh

sheep

a

apple

ee

ck

"Write the letter or letter pair that makes the _____ sound."

free

free	luck	queen
heel	whiz	bee
her	quack	quick
chips	chilly	lock
steeper	feet	rancher

Word Reading

▶ "Sound these out and say them fast."

"What sound does _____ **start** with?"

"What sound(s) does _____ **end** with?"

"What is the **middle/ vowel** sound in _____?"

"Now you spell _____."

Choose three words for student to spell and read.

my	want	what
there	she	over
by	they	saw
you'll	for	my

Dictate four sight words for student to spell and read.

▶ *"Read these sentences. Point to each word."*

My green frog fell in the dish and got all wet. My dad helped me mop up.

vowels: a, e, i, o, u

c<u>a</u>ne	c<u>a</u>n	k<u>i</u>t	k<u>i</u>te
h<u>o</u>p	h<u>o</u>pe	t<u>a</u>pe	t<u>a</u>p
b<u>i</u>te	b<u>i</u>t	r<u>o</u>b	r<u>o</u>be
c<u>u</u>te	c<u>u</u>t	<u>u</u>se	<u>u</u>s

Magic -e-

▶ "Here is the rule: If a word has an <u>e</u> at the end, the middle vowel says its name and the <u>e</u> is quiet. Let's practice this rule."

▶ "Is there an <u>e</u> at the end of this word? Will the middle vowel say its name or its sound?"

▶ "Let's sound out the word."

▶ "The magic -e- can make the <u>u</u> say /oo/ or /y/ /oo/. Sometimes you have to try both to see which fits."

y

Word Endings

▶ *Point to the y:*

"I'm going to say <u>kit</u> with this ending. <u>Kitty</u>."

"Your turn. Touch the <u>y</u> and say <u>kit</u> with this ending."

▶ *Repeat with:*

stick	spot
Dan	chub

▶ "Now you read these words."

fun	funny	sand	sandy
Tam	Tammy	Jim	Jimmy
lump	lumpy	yuck	yucky

Pair Practice

▶ "Let's do extra practice with our new letter pairs."

Tutor dictate: "Write the letters that make these sounds."

ck	ee	er
sw	sl	fl

slick   fern   sweeter

▶ "Now read these words."

pest   sheet   shack

"Now spell these words."

slack	stern	teen
rest	sweet	chick

meck   cheef   sherg

▶ "Now read these nonwords."

plack   verch   thert

"Now spell these nonwords."

sluck	fleest	flam

(See the Additional Supplementary Reading Scope and Sequence in the *Tutor Handbook* for additional titles.)

Book Reading

▶ Read *The Swimmers*.

Supplementary:
  Read *Floppy Mop*.

ou

cloud

Say the Sounds

▶ "Point to each letter or letter pair. Say the sound."

▶ "Ou is our new vowel team. The two vowels together make **one** sound, /ou/."

▶ "Tr makes **two** sounds."

ou	v	sw	ee
	vet	swim	tree

ch	c	ou	ck
cherry	cat		truck

u	ee	l	w
up		lion	window

er	ou	ck	tr
fern			train

ee	v	u	ou

"Write the letter or letter pair that makes the _____ sound."

shouted

outer	ouch	trout
shouted	chilly	straps
round	licked	couch
rusty	south	limps
hound	tricked	free

Word Reading

▶ "Sound these out and say them fast."

"What sound does _____ **start** with?"

"What sound(s) does _____ **end** with?"

"What is the **middle/ vowel** sound in _____?"

"Now you spell _____."

Choose three words for student to spell and read.

house	mouse

my	by	house
want	mouse	my
saw	house	what
want	over	there

▶ "This word is _____."

"You read it."

"Point and spell."

"What word?"

▶ *Have student read, point and spell, and then reread each word.*

Dictate four sight words for student to spell and read.

▶ "Read these sentences. Point to each word."

Come over to my house. There is a fast mouse. I'll get it to run by my bed.

chip	trip
chap	trap
trick	chick
champ	tramp

▶ "Some words with similar sounds are spelled differently. Listen to the beginning sounds in these pairs."

▶ "The tr letter pair can sound a lot like /ch/.

"Listen carefully to these word pairs. Then spell the words."

truck	chuck
chin	trim
trot	trust

vowels: a, e, i, o, u

m<u>a</u>t	m<u>a</u>te	k<u>i</u>t	k<u>i</u>te
d<u>i</u>me	S<u>a</u>m	b<u>i</u>ke	r<u>o</u>pe
c<u>a</u>t	c<u>a</u>ve	t<u>u</u>b	t<u>u</u>be

Magic -e-

▶ "Here is the rule: If a word has an e at the end, the middle vowel says its name and the e is quiet. Let's practice this rule."

▶ "Is there an e at the end of this word? Will the middle vowel say its name or its sound?"

▶ "Let's sound out the word."

Pair Practice

▶ "Let's do extra practice with our new letter pairs."

Tutor dictate: "Write the letters that make these sounds."

| ee | ou | ck |
| er | sw | tr |

| trip | steel | south |
| shout | term | track |

▶ "Now read these words."

"Now spell these words."

| flip | trick | speed |
| slack | peel | trout |

| trouf | cheeb | swerp |
| stoug | flast | swack |

▶ "Now read these nonwords."

"Now spell these nonwords."

| swout | treeb | cherf |

(See the Additional Supplementary Reading Scope and Sequence in the *Tutor Handbook* for additional titles.)

Book Reading

▶ Read *The Swimmers.*

Supplementary:
Read *Floppy Mop.*

ue

blue

Say the Sounds

▶ "Ue is our new vowel team. The two vowels together make **one** sound, /oo/."

▶ "Point to each letter or letter pair. Say the sound."

ue	ck	ou	h
	tru**ck**	cloud	hat
ee	t	ee	y
tree	table		yellow
ue	ck	qu	er
		queen	fern
ck	ou	ue	sw
			swim
tr	j	wh	ck
train	jet	whale	

blue

blue	sifter	pouch
coffee	couch	glue
wham	due	sixteen
clue	ground	cloudy
deeper	with	thunder

by	she	saw
want	house	my
mouse	were	what
there	they	over

Word Reading

▶ "Sound these out and say them fast."

"What sound does _____ **start** with?"

"What sound(s) does _____ **end** with?"

"What is the **middle/ vowel** sound in _____?"

"Now you spell _____."

Choose three words for student to spell and read.

Sight Words

▶ *Have student read, point and spell, and then reread each word.*

Dictate four sight words for student to spell and read.

My pet mouse is over there by the tree. I call her Teeny—she is quite small.

chip   trip

tramp   champ

chap   trap

▶ "Read these sentences. Point to each word."

Spelling Similar Sounds

▶ "Some words with similar sounds are spelled differently. Listen to the beginning sounds in these pairs."

▶ "The tr letter pair can sound a lot like /ch/, as in chain and train."

"Listen carefully to these word pairs. Then spell the words."

trap	chap
trick	chick
champ	tramp

vowels: a, e, i, o, u

mate	kite	Mit	came
slime	slim	same	shame
cut	cute	rob	robe
tip	dime	tap	bake

y

Tim	Timmy	sun	sunny
fish	fishy	pen	penny
pop	poppy	luck	lucky

Magic -e-

▶ "Here is the rule: If a word has an e at the end, the middle vowel says its name and the e is quiet. Let's practice this rule."

▶ "Is there an e at the end of this word? Will the middle vowel say its name or its sound?"

▶ "Let's sound out the word."

Word Endings

▶ *Point to the y:*

"I'm going to say kit with this ending. Kitty."

"Your turn. Touch the y and say kit with this ending."

▶ *Repeat with:*

bump	chop
run	sand

▶ "Now you read these words."

true   quick   south

week   herd   due

▶ "Now read these words."

"Now spell these words."

glue	swish	Bert
queen	true	shout

plue   deek   swerf

choug   pler   trest

▶ "Now read these nonwords."

"Now spell these nonwords."

smue	trib	flerb

(See the Additional Supplementary Reading Scope and Sequence in the *Tutor Handbook* for additional titles.)

Book Reading

▶ Read *Summer*.

Supplementary:
    Read *Lolly Pops*.

Mastery Test 5

Use with Mastery Test 5—Tester Recording Sheet (see *Tutor Handbook*).

Sounds

▶ "Point to each letter or letter pair and say the sound."

qu	fl	sk
sl	er	ee
st	ck	ou
tr	ue	sw

(Provide student with Mastery Test 5—Student Recording Sheet found in *Tutor Handbook*.)

✎ "Write the letters that make the _____ sound."

Word Reading

▶ "Sound these words out, then read them fast."

quilt	skid	sheet
hunter	swims	whiz
flash	skip	fern
need	slash	luck
couch	outer	glue

(Provide student with Mastery Test 5—Student Recording Sheet found in *Tutor Handbook*.)

Spelling

✎ "I say the word, and you write the word."

over   mouse   she   by

she's   my   house   want

Sight Word Reading

▶ "Read these words."

ew

screw

Say the Sounds

▶ "Point to each letter or letter pair. Say the sound."

▶ "The letter pair ew has **two** sounds: /oo/ as in new, and /y/ /oo/ as in few. You have to see which sounds right."

ew	sk	l	ou
	skunk	lion	cloud
ee	ue	ew	sk
tree	blue		
ck	sl	ew	ou
truck	slide		
er	ue	n	qu
fern		nail	queen
ou	ew	ue	ee

"Write the letter or letter pair that makes the _____ sound(s)."

new

new	cloud	our
blue	crew	teeth
found	drew	weeds
dew	out	stew
much	sound	glue

▶ "Sound these out and say them fast."

"What sound does _____ **start** with?"

"What sound(s) does _____ **end** with?"

"What is the **middle/ vowel** sound in _____?"

"Now you spell _____."

Choose three words for student to spell and read.

Tutor Notes *Always have student repeat/say the word before spelling. Always have student read all words after spelling them.*

any	many

Sight Words

▶ "This word is _____."

"You read it."

"Point and spell."

"What word?"

▶ *Have student read, point and spell, and then reread each word.*

by	she	any
or	was	want
many	mouse	house
my	she	was

▶ "Read these sentences. Point to each word."

Many cats creep in the weeds by the house, or over on the hill. They sit there. They hope for any mouse to come by.

trill   chill

champ   tramp

trim   chin

Lesson 51 cont'd

Spelling Similar Sounds

▶ "Some words with similar sounds are spelled differently. Listen to the beginning sounds in these pairs."

▶ "The tr letter pair can sound a lot like /ch/, as in trill and chill."

▶ "Listen carefully to these word pairs. Then spell the words."

trick	chick
chuck	truck
trap	chap

---

vowels: a, e, i, o, u

not   nose   like   lit

base   hat   tub   tube

gap   home   hop   bike

Magic -e-

▶ "Here is the rule: If a word has an e at the end, the middle vowel says its name and the e is quiet. Let's practice this rule."

▶ "Is there an e at the end of this word? Will the middle vowel say its name or its sound?"

▶ "Let's sound out the word."

▶ "Let's do extra practice with our new letter pairs."

Tutor dictate: "Write the letters that make these sounds."

ue	ew	ou
er	tr	ee

stew	true	mouth
her	sweep	dew

▶ "Now read these words."

"Now spell these words."

neck	new	seen
jerk	shout	flew

derp	rew	swen
goub	treem	chuf

▶ "Now read these nonwords."

"Now spell these nonwords."

lue	vert	thew

(See the Additional Supplementary Reading Scope and Sequence in the *Tutor Handbook* for additional titles.)

Book Reading

▶ Read *Summer*.

Supplementary:
Read *Lolly Pops*.

ew

scr<u>ew</u>

Say the Sounds

▶ "Point to each letter or letter pair. Say the sound."

▶ "Remember, the letter pair <u>ew</u> has **two** sounds: /oo/ as in <u>new</u>, and /y/ /oo/ as in <u>few</u>. You have to see which sounds right."

ou	ee	ck	ue
cloud	tree	tru<u>ck</u>	blue
qu	ew	wh	ou
queen		whale	
sh	ee	th	ew
sheep		thumb	
er	ou	ew	ch
fern			cherry
ue	ee	th	ou

"Write the letter or letter pair that makes the _____ sound."

Use all letter sounds for spelling.

flew

faster	slam	slap
grew	snap	our
flip	clue	wheels
shout	flop	flour
quacks	cloudy	true

Word Reading

► "Sound these out and say them fast."

"What sound does _____ **start** with?"

"What sound(s) does _____ **end** with?"

"What is the **middle/ vowel** sound in _____?"

NEW!

Choose six difficult words.

"Now you spell _____."

"Underline the letter pair(s) or word part(s) you know in the word."

head

or	by	she
head	want	house
over	many	head
any	saw	what

Sight Words

▶ "This word is _____."

"You read it."

"Point and spell."

"What word?"

NEW!

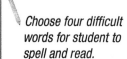

Choose four difficult words for student to spell and read.

▶ "Read these sentences. Point to each word."

My cat sits by my dog's head when she sleeps. If a mouse runs by, my cat will chase it. Then my dog will wake up!

vowels: a, e, i, o, u

n<u>o</u>t	n<u>o</u>se	c<u>u</u>te	c<u>u</u>t
b<u>a</u>se	b<u>a</u>t	k<u>i</u>t	k<u>i</u>te
g<u>a</u>me	g<u>a</u>p	m<u>o</u>pe	m<u>o</u>p
h<u>o</u>me	w<u>o</u>ke	p<u>e</u>t	P<u>e</u>te

Magic -e-

▶ "Here is the rule: If a word has an <u>e</u> at the end, the middle vowel says its name and the <u>e</u> is quiet. Use the rule to read these words."

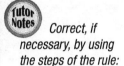 *Correct, if necessary, by using the steps of the rule:*

"Is there an <u>e</u> at the end of this word? Will the middle vowel say its name or its sound?"

"Remember, the magic -e- can make the <u>u</u> say /oo/ or /y/ /oo/. Sometimes you have to try both to see which fits."

▶ "Let's do extra practice with our new letter pairs."

✎ *Tutor dictate:* "Write the letters that make these sounds."

ew	sh	ou
fl	er	tr

flew	flour	term

▶ "Now read these words."

speech	Sue	crew

✎ "Now spell these words."

brew	trout	couch
blue	clerk	teeth

outh	zerp	sweeb

▶ "Now read these nonwords."

troush	zew	mert

✎ "Now spell these nonwords."

flez	terch	shoug

(See the Additional Supplementary Reading Scope and Sequence in the *Tutor Handbook* for additional titles.)

Book Reading

▶ Read *Cat and Mouse*.

-y

fly

Say the Sounds

▶ "Point to each letter or letter pair. Say the sound."

▶ "When y is at the end of a word, it can sound like the letter name i, or like the letter name e."

ew	ou	-y	ck
scr<u>ew</u>	cloud		tru<u>ck</u>

er	-y	qu	ew
fern		queen	

ue	th	er	ck
blue	thumb		

ou	-y	qu	th

er	ew	ue	ou

"Write the letter or letter pair that makes the _____ sound."

Use all letter sounds for spelling.

dry

drew	try	my
shout	cry	newer
shy	stew	true
steel	sky	grew
flour	cloud	faster

Word Reading

▶ "Sound these out and say them fast."

Choose six difficult words.

"Now you spell _____."

"Underline the letter pair(s) or word part(s) you know in the word."

"Read the word."

knew

head	knew	she
any	want	knew
head	house	was
over	what's	knew

▶ "This word is _____."

"You read it."

"Point and spell."

"What word?"

"Read each word."

Choose four difficult words for student to spell and read.

▶ "Read these sentences. Point to each word."

"I knew it," he said. "I knew what the <u>answer</u> was. But the game was over by that time."

vowels: a, e, i, o, u

c<u>u</u>te   c<u>a</u>pe   h<u>a</u>te   c<u>u</u>t

c<u>a</u>p   m<u>a</u>ke   h<u>a</u>t   w<u>o</u>ke

t<u>i</u>p   t<u>a</u>pe   w<u>i</u>n   w<u>i</u>ne

pl<u>a</u>n   pl<u>a</u>ne   p<u>i</u>ne   p<u>i</u>n

Magic -e-

▶ "Let's say the magic -e- rule: If a word has an <u>e</u> at the end, the middle vowel says its name and the <u>e</u> is quiet. Use the rule to read these words."

Tutor Notes *Correct, if necessary, by using the steps of the rule:*

"Is there an <u>e</u> at the end of this word? Will the middle vowel say its name or its sound?"

"Remember, the magic -e- can make the <u>u</u> say /oo/ or /y/ /oo/. Sometimes you have to try both to see which fits."

cute	fuse	mute
tune	tube	dune
cube	flute	mule

NEW! Long u Sounds

▶ "Remember, the magic -e- can make the u say **one** sound, /oo/ as in tune, or it can make **two** sounds, /y/ /oo/, as in cute."

▶ "Let's read these magic -e- words and listen to the long u sound."

▶ *For each word:*

"Read the word."

"What sound does the u make?"

feet

scout

clerk

fern

true

chew

- -

sheed

therm

gouch

jeth

smer

drick

(See the Additional Supplementary Reading Scope and Sequence in the *Tutor Handbook* for additional titles.)

▶ "Let's do extra practice with our new letter pairs."

Tutor dictate: "Write the letters that make these sounds."

er	ou	ee
th	ew	ue

▶ "Now read these words."

"Now spell these words."

bound	term	sheet
slouch	glue	brew

▶ "Now read these nonwords."

"Now spell these nonwords."

swert	thoud	merk

Book Reading

▶ Read *Cat and Mouse*.

−y

fly

ew	ou	−y	ck
scr<u>ew</u>	cloud		tru<u>ck</u>

er	qu	ee	ch
fern	queen	tree	cherry

−y	wh	ue	sh
	whale	blue	sheep

Say the Sounds

▶ "Point to each letter or letter pair. Say the sound."

▶ "Remember, when <u>y</u> is at the end of a word, it can sound like the letter name <u>i</u>, or like the letter name <u>e</u>."

"Write the letter or letter pair that makes the _____ sound."

Use all letter sounds for spelling.

dry	sound	newest
track	chew	cry
tricked	my	litter
rounder	loud	stew
try	packed	supply

Word Reading

▶ "Sound these out and say them fast."

Choose six difficult words.

"Now you spell _____."

"Underline the letter pair(s) or word part(s) you know in the word."

"Read the word."

know

knew	over	was
head	want	know
any	was	knew
she	over	head

"I know that I saw a big bug on the wall over my bed. It was over my head. My mom helped me <u>put</u> it in a cup and take it outside."

▶ "Read these sentences. Point to each word."

vowels: a, e, i, o, u

mate	mat	fat	fate
cape	cap	shin	shine
plan	plane	twine	twin
Sam	same	bit	bite

Magic -e-

▶ "Let's say the magic -e- rule: If a word has an e at the end, the middle vowel says its name and the e is quiet. Use the rule to read these words."

tutor Notes *Correct, if necessary, by using the steps of the rule:*

"Is there an e at the end of this word? Will the middle vowel say its name or its sound?"

"Remember, the magic -e- is quiet."

cute   fume   prune

flute   mule   June

crude   tube   cube

The Long u Sounds

▶ "Remember, the magic -e- can make the u say **one** sound, /oo/ as in tune, or it can make **two** sounds, /y/ /oo/, as in cute."

▶ "Let's read these magic-e- words and listen to the long u sound."

▶ *For each word:*

"Read the word."

"What sound does the u make?"

Pair Practice

▶ "Let's do extra practice with our new letter pairs."

🖉 *Tutor dictate:* "Write the letters that make these sounds."

ew	ou	ck
er	qu	ue

queen   ouch   jeep

shout   sweet   check

▶ "Now read these words."

🖉 "Now spell these words."

quiz	click	cloud
flew	joust	deck

berg   flouz   slew

leck   deev   sheef

▶ "Now read these nonwords."

🖉 "Now spell these nonwords."

glack   newp   sterf

(See the Additional Supplementary Reading Scope and Sequence in the *Tutor Handbook* for additional titles.)

Book Reading

▶ Read *Bud's Nap.*

ar

car

Say the Sounds

▶ "Point to each letter or letter pair. Say the sound."

ew	ou	–y	ck
scr<u>ew</u>	cloud	fl<s>y</s>	tru<u>ck</u>

ar	ew	wh	ue
		whale	blue

er	ee	ar	ew
fern	tree		

"Write the letter or letter pair that makes the _____ sound."

Use all letter sounds for spelling.

shy	white	hard
yarn	crew	tart
barn	tricked	try
cheek	hunter	slick
stew	why	when

Choose six difficult words.

"Now you spell _____."

"Underline the letter pair(s) or word part(s) you know in the word."

"Read the word."

have

head   knew   have

any   some   know

have   head   was

many   knew   house

Sight Words

▶ "This word is _____."

"You read it."

"Point and spell."

"What word?"

"Read each word."

Choose four difficult words for student to spell and read.

We have lemonade when it is <u>warm</u>. And we bake cupcakes when we have a party!

▶ "Read these sentences. Point to each word."

vowels: a, e, i, o, u

pl<u>a</u>te	pl<u>a</u>t	tr<u>i</u>p	tr<u>i</u>be
sl<u>i</u>me	sl<u>i</u>m	sp<u>i</u>t	sp<u>i</u>te
T<u>i</u>m	t<u>i</u>me	m<u>a</u>te	m<u>a</u>t

▶ "Let's say the magic -e- rule: If a word has an <u>e</u> at the end, the middle vowel says its name and the <u>e</u> is quiet. Use the rule to read these words."

 Tutor Notes *Correct by using the steps of the rule:*

"Is there an <u>e</u> at the end of this word? Will the middle vowel say its name or its sound?"

---

ing

Word Endings

▶ *Point to the ing:* "I'm going to say sit with this ending. Sitting."

▶ "Words that end in <u>ing</u> describe something that is going on now."

▶ "Your turn. Touch the <u>ing</u> and say <u>sit</u> with this ending."

▶ *Repeat with:*

fish	hit
hop	make

▶ "Now you read these words."

sit	sitting	wish	wishing
jump	jumping	clap	clapping

"If a word has one vowel and ends with one consonant, we double the last consonant and then add the <u>ing</u>."

cube	prune	duke
tube	rude	tune
cute	mule	fuse

Long u Sounds

▶ "Remember, the magic -e- can make the u say **one** sound, /oo/ as in tune, or it can make **two** sounds, /y/ /oo/, as in cute."

▶ "Let's read these magic-e- words and listen to the long u sound."

▶ *For each word:*

"Read the word."

"What sound does the u make?"

start flock couch

stew path hard

arp bouf snew

sherp blark smick

(See the Additional Supplementary Reading Scope and Sequence in the *Tutor Handbook* for additional titles.)

Pair Practice

▶ "Let's do extra practice with our new letter pairs."

Tutor dictate: "Write the letters that make these sounds."

ew	ar	ou
er	ck	ue

▶ "Now read these words."

"Now spell these words."

blew	spark	smart
stout	quack	clock

▶ "Now read these nonwords."

"Now spell these nonwords."

jart	frew	starp

Book Reading

▶ Read *Bud's Nap*.

ar

car

ew	ch	ar	-y
scr<u>ew</u>	cherry		fl<s>y</s>

ou	sh	wh	ck
cloud	sheep	whale	tru<u>ck</u>

ee	er	th	ou
tree	fern	thumb	

---

market	same	start
chew	scar	jar
darker	parking	trout
grime	feet	try
threw	slouch	whine

Say the Sounds

▶ "Point to each letter or letter pair. Say the sound."

"Write the letter or letter pair that makes the _____ sound."

Use all letter sounds for spelling.

Word Reading

▶ "Sound these out and say them fast."

Choose six difficult words.

"Now you spell _____."

"Underline the letter pair(s) or word part(s) you know in the word."

"Read the word."

Sight Words

▶ "Read each word."

have	head	knew
was	over	she
know	saw	have
my	want	by
or	they	all
there	what	come
to	for	into
were	said	have
any	many	mouse
some	she's	you'll

Choose eight difficult words for the student to spell and read.

I know I have five dimes.
They are in my house.
I can spend them on a
bag of chips.

▶ "Read these sentences. Point to each word."

vowels: a, e, i, o, u

Magic -e-

▶ "Let's say the magic -e- rule: If a word has an e at the end, the middle vowel says its name and the e is quiet. Use the rule to read these words."

sh<u>a</u>le   sh<u>a</u>ft   cr<u>i</u>mp   cr<u>i</u>me

cr<u>a</u>ne   cr<u>a</u>m   st<u>a</u>le   st<u>i</u>ll

m<u>a</u>te   pl<u>a</u>ne   t<u>i</u>me   pl<u>a</u>nt

Tutor Notes *Correct by using the steps of the rule:*

"Is there an e at the end of this word? Will the middle vowel say its name or its sound?"

ing

fit   fitting   stop   stopping

tap   tapping   shout   shouting

▶ *Point to the ing:* "I'm going to say <u>sit</u> with this ending. <u>Sitting</u>."

▶ "Words that end in <u>ing</u> describe something that is going on now."

▶ "Your turn. Touch the <u>ing</u> and say <u>sit</u> with this ending."

▶ *Repeat with:*

smile   eat

jump   write

▶ "Now you read these words."

"If a word has one vowel and ends with one consonant, we double the last consonant and then add the <u>ing</u>."

fume	dune	June
flute	mule	cute
prune	fuse	rude

Long u Sounds

▶ "Remember, the magic -e- can make the <u>u</u> say **one** sound, /oo/ as in <u>tune</u>, or it can make **two** sounds, /y/ /oo/, as in <u>cute</u>."

▶ "Let's read these magic-e- words and listen to the long <u>u</u> sound."

▶ *For each word:*

"Read the word."

"What sound does the <u>u</u> make?"

▶ "Let's do extra practice with our new letter pairs."

Tutor dictate: "Write the letters that make these sounds."

ar	ew	ou
sw	ue	er

bark   brew   cloud

sweep   term   yard

▶ "Now read these words."

"Now spell these words."

mark	fern	mouth
threw	yarn	true

yarp   spart   mout

vert   flar   clewf

▶ "Now read these nonwords."

"Now spell these nonwords."

swerf	joud	mam

(See the Additional Supplementary Reading Scope and Sequence in the *Tutor Handbook* for additional titles.)

Book Reading

▶ Read *The Red Car*.

ar
car

ew
scr<u>ew</u>

ch
cherry

sh
sheep

Say the Sounds

▶ "Point to each letter or letter pair. Say the sound."

▶ "<u>Gr</u> makes **two** sounds."

▶ "<u>Sn</u> makes **two** sounds."

ee
tree

ck
tru<u>ck</u>

ar

ou
cloud

ar

th
thumb

qu
queen

ew

gr
grape

fl
flower

tr
train

sn
snail

"Write the letter or letter pair that makes the _____ sound."

Use all letter sounds for spelling.

start   sharp   trout

cheek   flew   quick

green   trick   outing

snout   queen   snack

stewing   flicker   grin

Word Reading

▶ "Sound these out and say them fast."

Choose six difficult words.

"Now you spell _____."

"Underline the letter pair(s) or word part(s) you know in the word."

"Read the word."

two

one

have   know   two

knew   she   one

head   knew   saw

Sight Words

▶ "This word is _____."

"You read it."

"Point and spell."

"What word?"

"Read each word."

Choose four difficult words for student to spell and read.

I saw two dogs ride by in that car! One was looking out at us. I saw the car drive in a parking lot.

▶ "Read these sentences. Point to each word."

igh

sigh   tighter   thighs

high   sunlight   slightly

mighty   sighing   highest

NEW!
Useful Word Chunks

▶ "This chunk is _____."

"Read, spell, and read."

"By learning this chunk, you can read and spell lots of words."

▶ "Read and spell these words."

vowels: a, e, i, o, u

plane	cap	plan	base
game	nose	Cam	came
spine	splint	slime	slim

▶ "Let's say the magic -e- rule: If a word has an e at the end, the middle vowel says its name and the e is quiet. Use the rule to read these words."

Tutor Notes *Correct by using the steps of the rule:*

"Is there an e at the end of this word? Will the middle vowel say its name or its sound?"

y

Word Endings

▶ *Review: Point to the y:* "I'm going to say kit with this ending. Kitty."

▶ "Your turn. Touch the y and say kit with this ending."

▶ *Repeat with:*

| stick | spot |
| Dan | chub |

▶ "Now you read these words."

| fun | funny | sand | sandy |
| Tam | Tammy | Jim | Jimmy |

sharf   flert   groum

snoub   greep   sharf

(See the Additional Supplementary Reading Scope and Sequence in the *Tutor Handbook* for additional titles.)

Pair Practice

NEW!

▶ "From now on, this will be practice with nonwords only."

▶ "Now read these nonwords."

"Now spell these nonwords."

  sneef groub tharp

Book Reading

▶ Read *The Red Car*.

ow

clown

Say the Sounds

▶ "Point to each letter or letter pair. Say the sound."

▶ "The letter pair <u>ow</u> makes a gliding sound, /ow/."

ar	–y	ow	ew
car	fl<s>y</s>		scr<u>ew</u>

ue	ow	ar	ck
blue			tru<u>ck</u>

ou	ue	ee	ow
cloud		tree	

"Write the letter or letter pair that makes the _____ sound."

Use all letter sounds for spelling.

Word Reading

▶ "Sound these out and say them fast."

started	arm	flower
chow	brow	grew
chart	power	artist
army	wow	newer
plow	spark	true

Choose six difficult words.

"Now you spell _____."

"Underline the letter pair(s) or word part(s) you know in the word."

"Read the word."

live

▶ "This word is _____."

"You read it."

"Point and spell."

"What word?"

"Read each word."

two	live	one
have	know	two
one	live	knew
was	want	live

Choose four difficult words for student to spell and read.

▶ "Read these sentences. Point to each word."

Didn't you live in a house over by the park when you were two? How did you like the brown slide and swings in the park?

ight

sight	flight	light
tight	night	right
bright	might	slight

Lesson 58 cont'd

Useful Word Chunks

▶ "This chunk is _____."

"Read, spell, and read."

"By learning this chunk, you can read and spell lots of words."

▶ "Read and spell these words."

---

vowels: a, e, i, o, u

flame	flag	strip	stripe
chin	chime	mope	mop
mule	mile	blade	bled
file	fuse	game	grime

Magic -e-

▶ "Let's say the magic -e- rule: If a word has an e at the end, the middle vowel says its name and the e is quiet. Use the rule to read these words."

Tutor Notes *Correct by using the steps of the rule:*

"Is there an e at the end of this word? Will the middle vowel say its name or its sound?"

"Remember, the magic -e- can make the u say /oo/ or /y/ /oo/. Sometimes you have to try both to see which fits."

gow   doup   snart

cherm   sperf   varm

(See the Additional Supplementary Reading Scope and Sequence in the *Tutor Handbook* for additional titles.)

Pair Practice

▶ "Read these nonwords."

"Now spell these nonwords."

smue   snowl   cleth

Book Reading

▶ Read *Max and the Tom Cats*.

ow

clown

ar	gr	ue	ow
car		blue	
	grape		
ck	er	ow	ue
truck	fern		blue
ew	ou	ow	ar
scr<u>ew</u>	cloud		

Say the Sounds

▶ "Point to each letter or letter pair. Say the sound."

▶ "The letter pair <u>ow</u> makes a gliding sound, /ow/."

"Write the letter or letter pair that makes the _____ sound."

Use all letter sounds for spelling.

tower	charm	shower
chow	ark	power
how	starter	barking
weeds	howl	wish
ground	arch	try

Word Reading

▶ "Sound these out and say them fast."

Choose six difficult words.

"Now you spell _____."

"Underline the letter pair(s) or word part(s) you know in the word."

"Read the word."

very

one	very	have
two	know	saw
live	very	was
two	one	very

Sight Words

▶ "This word is _____."

"You read it."

"Point and spell."

"What word?"

"Read each word."

Choose four difficult words for student to spell and read.

▶ "Read these sentences. Point to each word."

If you are very <u>good</u> tonight, you can have one of my flowers. I know that you like them.

igh

ight

high	bright	brighter
flight	sight	light
tonight	night	sunlight
right	tighten	skylight

▶ "Point to each box. Read and spell each chunk."

▶ "Read and spell these words."

---

vowels: a, e, i, o, u

grime	broke	brat	grin
split	spoke	male	mine
mint	quite	note	stun
stone	stand	stake	stack

Magic -e-

▶ "Let's say the magic -e- rule: If a word has an e at the end, the middle vowel says its name and the e is quiet. Use the rule to read these words."

 *Correct by using the steps of the rule:*

"Is there an e at the end of this word? Will the middle vowel say its name or its sound?"

trow   groud   snew

karm   zerl   verk

(See the Additional Supplementary Reading Scope and Sequence in the *Tutor Handbook* for additional titles.)

Pair Practice

▶ "Read these nonwords."

"Now spell these nonwords."

wark   sneef   groust

Book Reading

▶ Read *Max and the Tom Cats*.

al

salt

ew	ou	ue	al
scr<u>ew</u>	cloud	blue	

ar	ee	al	ew
car	tree		

al	wh	ow	ck
	whale	clown	tru<u>ck</u>

now	calm	ball
flower	army	high
farmer	salty	harp
brighter	crowd	stall
loudest	threw	shower

Say the Sounds

▶ "Point to each letter or letter pair. Say the sound."

▶ "Note that the letter pair <u>al</u> and the word <u>all</u> sound the same! The /al/ sound can be spelled with <u>l</u> or <u>ll</u>."

✎ "Write the letter or letter pair that makes the _____ sound."

Use all letter sounds for spelling.

Word Reading

▶ "Sound these out and say them fast."

✎ *Choose six difficult words.*

"Now you spell _____."

"Underline the letter pair(s) or word part(s) you know in the word."

"Read the word."

says

have	two	one
says	very	knew
head	says	very
one	have	live

▶ "This word is _____."

"You read it."

"Point and spell."

"What word?"

"Read each word."

Choose four difficult words for student to spell and read.

She says I have just two cats. She <u>does</u> not know that I have three. One is brown, one is white, and one is very, very smart!

▶ "Read these sentences. Point to each word."

vowels: a, e, i, o, u

n<u>o</u>se	sp<u>i</u>ke	b<u>a</u>se	b<u>e</u>st
sn<u>a</u>ck	sn<u>a</u>ke	l<u>a</u>ke	l<u>a</u>ck
gr<u>i</u>me	m<u>a</u>ke	sk<u>i</u>t	b<u>e</u>nt

ing

wish	wishing	hit	hitting
limp	limping	win	winning

Magic -e-

► "Let's say the magic -e- rule: If a word has an <u>e</u> at the end, the middle vowel says its name and the <u>e</u> is quiet. Use the rule to read these words."

Tutor Notes *Correct by using the steps of the rule:*

"Is there an <u>e</u> at the end of this word? Will the middle vowel say its name or its sound?"

Word Endings

► *Point to the* <u>ing</u>*:* "I'm going to say <u>sit</u> with this ending. <u>Sitting</u>."

► "Your turn. Touch the <u>ing</u> and say <u>sit</u> with this ending."

► *Repeat with:*

snow	fall
shop	pick

► "Now you read these words."

dalp   nart   spoug

skow   derm   talm

(See the Additional Supplementary Reading Scope and Sequence in the *Tutor Handbook* for additional titles.)

Pair Practice

▶ "Read these nonwords."

"Now spell these nonwords."

palt   snoup   greev

Book Reading

▶ Read *Willy's Wish.*

Supplementary:
    Read *Frogs.*

Mastery Test 6

Use with Mastery Text 6—Tester Recording Sheet (see *Tutor Handbook*).

Sounds

▶ "Point to each letter or letter pair and say the sound."

ew	–y	ar
ow	al	gr
ou	ue	ee
er	qu	tr

- -

🖉 "Write the letter(s) that makes the _____ sound."

(Provide student with Mastery Test 6—Student Recording Sheet found in *Tutor Handbook*.)

Word Reading

▶ "Sound these words out, then read them fast."

artist	wheeled	cry
hard	marker	stewing
brow	shy	shower
calm	salty	farmer
now	chart	bright

Spelling

🖉 "I say the word, and you write the word."

(Provide student with Mastery Test 6—Student Recording Sheet found in *Tutor Handbook*.)

any head knew have

live very says know

one many two house

**Sight Word
Reading**

▶ "Read these words."

al
salt

ow   ar   ew   al

clown   car   sc<u>rew</u>

ou   al   ee   ow

cloud   tree

al   ue   ar   er

     blue   fern

salty   taller   shouted

clue   outside   scald

outfit   bright   sunshine

brown   sheets   ballgame

sparkler   carpet   archer

Say the Sounds

▶ "Point to each letter pair. Say the sound."

▶ "Remember, the letter pair <u>al</u> and the word <u>all</u> sound the same! The /al/ sound can be spelled with <u>l</u> or <u>ll</u>."

"Write the letter pair that makes the _____ sound."

Choose three or more sounds for spelling.

Word Reading

▶ "Sound these out and say them fast."

Choose six difficult words.

"Now you spell _____."

"Underline the letter pair(s) or word part(s) you know in the word."

"Read the word."

▶ "Read each word."

says	very	one
two	live	have
know	saw	head
any	says	or
many	very	knew

Choose four difficult words for student to spell and read.

▶ "Read these sentences. Point to each word."

We saw one or two very tall trees in the yard. We knew that one was a pine tree and one was an elm tree. The pine was very green, and the elm was very brown.

moonlight   rainfall

ballpark   starfish

beehive   hillside

sailboat   pancake

---

vowels: a, e, i, o, u

s<u>a</u>le	st<u>i</u>ll	m<u>u</u>le	str<u>i</u>pe
T<u>i</u>m	t<u>i</u>me	sl<u>i</u>me	pl<u>a</u>te
sl<u>i</u>m	c<u>u</u>te	c<u>u</u>t	st<u>a</u>le

---

dalp   greeb   shouk

flet   snall   carg

(See the Additional Supplementary Reading Scope and Sequence in the *Tutor Handbook* for additional titles.)

NEW!
Reading Long Words

▶ "Long words are easy to read when we break them up into smaller words. All of these words are compound words. They are made of smaller words. Cover the end of the word, read the first part, then read the whole word."

Magic -e-

▶ "Let's say the magic -e- rule: if a word has an <u>e</u> at the end, the middle vowel says its name and the <u>e</u> is quiet. Use the rule to read these words."

Tutor Notes *Correct by using the steps of the rule:*

"Is there an <u>e</u> at the end of this word? Will the middle vowel say its name or its sound?"

Pair Practice

▶ "Read these nonwords."

✎ "Now spell these nonwords."

   treb   boust   snuv

Book Reading

▶ Read *Willy's Wish*.

ay
hay

Say the Sounds

▶ "Point to each letter pair. Say the sound."

▶ "The <u>ay</u> letter pair sounds like the letter name <u>a</u>, and is usually seen at the end of a word."

al	ow	ar	ay
salt	clown	car	

ew	ay	al	ar
scr<u>ew</u>			

ow	al	ay	ew

"Write the letter pair that makes the _____ sound."

Choose three or more sounds for spelling.

play	target	calm
newest	payday	stray
salty	barking	marker
highest	clay	daytime
smart	pinball	flew

Word Reading

▶ "Sound these out and say them fast."

Choose six difficult words.

"Now you spell _____."

"Underline the letter pair(s) or word part(s) you know in the word."

"Read the word."

Lesson 62 cont'd

don't

says	one	don't
very	have	two
don't	live	says
saw	very	don't

Don't you know what time it is? Kay wants us to be at her house by two. She's counting on us to be there.

hayride   Mayday

daylight   pinball

hallway   overdue

anyone   driveway

Lesson 62 cont'd

Reading Long Words

▶ "Long words are easy to read when we break them up into smaller words. All of these words are compound words. They are made of smaller words. Cover the end of the word, read the first part, then read the whole word."

Magic -e-

vowels: a, e, i, o, u

fr<u>a</u>me   br<u>o</u>ke   b<u>a</u>ck   w<u>i</u>de

sm<u>i</u>le   sl<u>i</u>m   c<u>a</u>ke   tr<u>a</u>ck

b<u>i</u>ke   tr<u>i</u>m   d<u>a</u>te   t<u>i</u>me

(See the Additional Supplementary Reading Scope and Sequence in the *Tutor Handbook* for additional titles.)

▶ "Let's say the magic -e- rule: If a word has an <u>e</u> at the end, the middle vowel says its name and the <u>e</u> is quiet. Use the rule to read these words."

Tutor Notes *Correct by using the steps of the rule:*

"Is there an <u>e</u> at the end of this word? Will the middle vowel say its name or its sound? Remember, the <u>e</u> is quiet."

Book Reading

▶ Read *Funny Bunny*.

ay
hay

ar — car
al — salt
ay
ue — blue

ew — screw
th — thumb
ou — cloud
ow — clown

er — fern
ay
ar
al

---

playground   sprayed   owl

true   sticky   always

newer   thing   skate

frighten   staying   perky

blue   marker   intern

Say the Sounds

▶ "Point to each letter pair. Say the sound."

▶ "The ay letter pair sounds like the letter name a, and is usually seen at the end of a word."

"Write the letter pair that makes the _____ sound."

Choose three or more sounds for spelling.

Word Reading

▶ "Sound these out and say them fast."

Choose six difficult words.

"Now you spell _____."

"Underline the letter pair(s) or word part(s) you know in the word."

"Read the word."

says	don't	have
saw	two	live
very	many	have
don't	one	know
want	any	don't

Choose four difficult words for student to spell and read.

▶ "Read these sentences. Point to each word."

"We will be home at two," he said to his mom. "Don't start dinner without me." He didn't want to miss dinner with his granddad.

playground   anytime

roundup   headlight

sometimes   campfire

ballpark   catfight

Lesson 63 cont'd

Reading Long Words

▶ "Long words are easy to read when we break them up into smaller words. All of these words are compound words. They are made of smaller words. Cover the end of the word, read the first part, then read the whole word."

---

vowels: a, e, i, o, u

flame   mile   mill   flint

tone   fuse   slip   shape

mule   Pete   pest   spine

Magic -e-

▶ "Let's say the magic -e- rule: If a word has an e at the end, the middle vowel says its name and the e is quiet. Use the rule to read these words."

Tutor Notes *Correct by using the steps of the rule:*

"Is there an e at the end of this word? Will the middle vowel say its name or its sound? Remember, the e is quiet."

(See the Additional Supplementary Reading Scope and Sequence in the *Tutor Handbook* for additional titles.)

Book Reading

▶ Read *Funny Bunny*.

broom

book

Say the Sounds

▶ "Point to each letter pair. Say the sound."

▶ "This is the <u>oo</u> vowel team. It has **two** sounds: /oo/ like in broom and /oo/ like in book."

oo broom	**ay** hay	**ar** car	**er** fern
ew scr<u>ew</u>	**oo** book	**ow** clown	**ou** cloud
ue blue	**oo** broom	**ar**	**oo** book

"Write the letter pair that makes the _____ sound."

Choose three or more sounds for spelling.

Word Reading

▶ "Sound these out and say them fast."

▶ "Notice that the /oo/ sound in room is the same as the long <u>u</u> sound!"

Choose six difficult words.

"Now you spell _____."

"Underline the letter pair(s) or word part(s) you know in the word."

"Read the word."

room	troops	hook
stewing	shout	boots
outside	tar	shook
clerk	cartoons	Sue
brewing	mighty	farming

their

says	don't	very
their	saw	live
one	their	don't
very	says	have

▶ "This word is _____."

"You read it."

"Point and spell."

"What word?"

"Read each word."

Choose four difficult words for student to spell and read.

▶ "Read these sentences. Point to each word."

Their dad says that they will have a new house. They want to live on a farm. Their dad says the new house will have a very big yard.

runway   bookstore

nightmare   starfish

anything   someone

fireman   freeway

(See the Additional Supplementary Reading Scope and Sequence in the *Tutor Handbook* for additional titles.)

vowels: a, e, i, o, u

frame   ship   shape   slip

bride   wide   slid   tire

slide   dome   wilt   wire

Reading Long Words

▶ "Long words are easy to read when we break them up into smaller words. All of these words are compound words. They are made of smaller words. Cover the end of the word, read the first part, then read the whole word."

Magic -e-

▶ "Let's say the magic -e- rule: If a word has an e̲ at the end, the middle vowel says its name and the e̲ is quiet. Use the rule to read these words."

 *Correct by using the steps of the rule:*

"Is there an e̲ at the end of this word? Will the middle vowel say its name or its sound? Remember, the e̲ is quiet."

Book Reading

▶ Read *Jumper and the Clown*.

ue blue	**ch** cherry	**th** thumb	**er** fern
ay hay	**oo** broom	**al** salt	**ow** clown
ar car	**ew** scr<u>ew</u>	**ee** tree	**ou** cloud
qu queen	**oo** book	**wh** whale	**sh** sheep

Say the Sounds

▶ "Point to each letter pair. Say the sound."

✎ "Write the letter pair that makes the _____ sound."

Use all letter sounds for spelling.

quicker	crook	wheels
thick	tooth	harsh
frowning	charts	tighten
hood	white	took
mark	layer	archer

Word Reading

▶ "Sound these out and say them fast."

✎ *Choose six difficult words.*

"Now you spell _____."

"Underline the letter pair(s) or word part(s) you know in the word."

"Read the word."

we've

we'll

Sight Words

their	we've	says
don't	we'll	very
we've	their	don't
any	says	we've

▶ "This word is _____."

  "You read it."

  "Point and spell."

  "What word?"

▶ "<u>We've</u> is a short way to say <u>we have</u>. <u>We'll</u> is a short way to say <u>we will</u>. This mark (') is called an apostrophe. We call these words contractions."

  "Read each word."

Choose four difficult words for student to spell and read.

▶ "Read these sentences. Point to each word."

We'll live in our same house, but we'll visit them in their new one. We've seen it two times.

▶ "Long words are made
of syllables and are
easy to read when we
break them up into
smaller chunks."

▶ "We can find the
syllables by looking
for and hearing the
vowels."

interesting
in ter est ing

▶ "This looks like a
difficult word until
we break it into four
syllables. See, each
syllable has a vowel.
When we say each
syllable, you can feel
your mouth open. Each
syllable has one beat."

in vest ed

car pen ter

pow er ful

▶ "First, read these long
words already broken
into syllables. Then
read the word fast."

infected   blistering   forgetful

▶ "Now break these
words into syllables,
read the syllables, and
then read the word."

Word Endings

▶ **Review**: *Point to the ing.*

"I'm going to say <u>sit</u> with this ending. <u>Sitting</u>."

"Your turn. Touch the <u>ing</u> and say <u>sit</u> with this ending."

▶ *Repeat with:*

brush	poke
fish	turn

```
ing
```

▶ "Now you add these endings to the words under them."

"Read each word."

"Say the word with the ending above it."

s	ed	ing	y
boot	bat	poke	cloud
hat	look	eat	chop
wing	rate	fish	mush
tray	turn	pack	star

(See the Additional Supplementary Reading Scope and Sequence in the *Tutor Handbook* for additional titles.)

Book Reading

▶ Read *Jumper and the Clown*.

oa

boat

Say the Sounds

▶ "Point to each letter pair. Say the sound."

▶ "The <u>oa</u> vowel team sounds like the letter name <u>o</u>."

oo broom	**ay** hay	**oa**	**al** salt
oa	**al**	**ay**	**ow** clown
al	**ow**	**oa**	**oo** book

"Write the letter pair that makes the _____ sound."

Choose three or more sounds for spelling.

Word Reading

▶ "Sound these out and say them fast."

boots	slight	salty
floated	player	toasty
frowning	clay	roasted
soapy	calm	lighter
malted	wallet	shook

Choose six difficult words.

"Now you spell _____."

"Underline the letter pair(s) or word part(s) you know in the word."

"Read the word."

who

their	don't	who
many	who	we've
two	have	their
who	very	don't

Lesson 66 cont'd

Sight Words

▶ "This word is _____."

"You read it."

"Point and spell."

"What word?"

▶ "We've is a short way to say we have. This mark (') is called an apostrophe. We call these words contractions."

"Read each word."

Choose four difficult words for student to spell and read.

▶ "Read these sentences. Point to each word."

Who likes to live on a farm?
A person who likes goats,
cows, chickens, and sheep.
I don't know many kids who
live on a farm.

▶ "Long words are made of syllables and are easy to read when we break them up into smaller chunks."

▶ "We can find the syllables by looking for and hearing the vowels."

disgusted
dis gust ed

▶ "This looks like a difficult word until we break it into three syllables. See, each syllable has a vowel. When we say each syllable, you can feel your mouth open. Each syllable has one beat."

un der stand

ten der foot

un clut ter

▶ "First, read these long words already broken into syllables. Then read the words fast."

insisting   lookout

headlines   schoolhouse

▶ "Now break these words into syllables, read the syllables, and then read the words."

(See the Additional Supplementary Reading Scope and Sequence in the *Tutor Handbook* for additional titles.)

Book Reading

▶ Read *Jumper and the Clown*.

oa

boat

oo	**ou**	**oa**	**ew**
broom	cloud		scr<u>ew</u>

ay	**ew**	**al**	**oa**
hay		salt	

oa	**oo**	**ou**	**al**
	book		

Say the Sounds

▶ "Point to each letter pair. Say the sound."

▶ "Remember, the <u>oa</u> vowel team sounds like the letter name <u>o</u>."

"Write the letter pair that makes the _____ sound."

Choose three or more sounds for spelling.

---

foamy	stamp	roasted
mushy	shouted	swaying
right	lumpy	stood
toasted	pray	cooled
chewy	bars	clouds

Word Reading

▶ "Sound these out and say them fast."

Choose six difficult words.

"Now you spell _____."

"Underline the letter pair(s) or word part(s) you know in the word."

"Read the word."

from	eyes

who	eyes	from
don't	live	any
we'll	from	eyes
have	who	from

▶ "This word is _____."

"You read it."

"Point and spell."

"What word?"

"Read each word."

Choose four difficult words for student to spell and read.

▶ "Read these sentences. Point to each word."

We went from my house to their house to have lunch. Don't ask me what we ate. I forget what it was called, but it was very good!

▶ "Long words are made of syllables and are easy to read when we break them up into smaller chunks."

▶ "We can find the syllables by looking for and hearing the vowels."

contacting

con tact ing

▶ "This looks like a difficult word until we break it into three syllables. See, each syllable has a vowel. When we say each syllable, you can feel your mouth open. Each syllable has one beat."

un der line

dis play ing

in ter rupt

▶ "First, read these long words already broken into syllables. Then read the word fast."

payment   firewood

interesting   backpacking

▶ "Now break these words into syllables, read the syllables, and then read the word."

ing

▶ *Review*: *Point to the ing.*

"I'm going to say sit with this ending. Sitting."

"Your turn. Touch the ing and say sit with this ending."

▶ *Repeat with:*

walk	hammer
work	think

s	ed	ing	y
brush	bat	poke	lump
hat	want	eat	chop
wing	rate	fish	fish
lunch	turn	turn	star

▶ "Now you add these endings to the words under them."

"Read each word."

"Say the word with the ending above it."

(See the Additional Supplementary Reading Scope and Sequence in the *Tutor Handbook* for additional titles.)

Book Reading

▶ Read *Samantha*.

ai

rain

Say the Sounds

▶ "Point to each letter or letter pair. Say the sound."

▶ "The ai vowel team sounds like the letter name a."

oa	ai	ay	oo
boat		hay	broom

ai	ar	ew	er
	car	scr<u>ew</u>	fern

oa	ai	ay	ou
			cloud

"Write the letter or letter pair that makes the _____ sound."

Choose three or more sounds for spelling.

Word Reading

▶ "Sound these out and say them fast."

rain	days	waiting
stray	sailing	paid
mail	tighten	failed
way	jail	plain
mermaid	spray	temper

Choose six difficult words.

"Now you spell _____."

"Underline the letter pair(s) or word part(s) you know in the word."

"Read the word."

are	aren't

eyes	from	who
are	aren't	don't
any	their	says
are	many	aren't

▶ "This word is _____."

"You read it."

"Point and spell."

"What word?"

▶ "<u>Aren't</u> is a short way to say <u>are not</u>. This mark (') is called an apostrophe. We call these words contractions."

"Read each word."

Choose four difficult words for student to spell and read.

▶ "Read these sentences. Point to each word."

We have the very best players on our side. Our coach says that they always try their best. They aren't always the winners, but they play hard.

Reading Long Words

▶ "Long words are made of syllables and are easy to read when we break them up into smaller chunks."

▶ "We can find the syllables by looking for and hearing the vowels."

---

unpainted

un paint ed

▶ "This looks like a difficult word until we break it into three syllables. See, each syllable has a vowel. When we say each syllable, you can feel your mouth open. Each syllable has one beat."

---

ex pand ing

hun dred

dis play ing

▶ "First, read these long words already broken into syllables. Then read the word fast."

---

inspectors   starlight

braided   contrasting

▶ "Now break these words into syllables, read the syllables, and then read the word."

(See the Additional Supplementary Reading Scope and Sequence in the *Tutor Handbook* for additional titles.)

Book Reading

▶ Read *Samantha*.

ai

rain

oa	**ai**	**ay**	**oo**
boat		hay	broom
al	**ow**	**ar**	**ew**
salt	clown	car	scr<u>ew</u>
ee	**er**	**ou**	**ue**
tree	fern	cloud	blue

Say the Sounds

▶ "Point to each letter pair. Say the sound."

▶ "Remember, the <u>ai</u> vowel team sounds like the letter name <u>a</u>."

"Write the letter pair that makes the _____ sound."

Choose three or more sounds for spelling.

stain	clay	tools
away	claim	play
strainer	tooth	gray
brain	flight	trail
frogs	painted	noon

Word Reading

▶ "Sound these out and say them fast."

Choose six difficult words.

"Now you spell _____."

"Underline the letter pair(s) or word part(s) you know in the word."

"Read the word."

no	so	go

are	no	from
go	don't	their
he	so	go
aren't	no	eyes
he	so	go

Sight Words

▶ "This word is _____."

"You read it."

"Point and spell."

"What word?"

"Read each word."

Choose four difficult words for student to spell and read.

▶ "Read these sentences. Point to each word."

Our new puppy likes to rip up our things. So we are training him by saying, "No. Don't go over there. Don't chew on my socks." Then I say, "Let's go out and play."

▶ "Long words are made of syllables and are easy to read when we break them up into smaller chunks."

▶ "We can find the syllables by looking for and hearing the vowels."

bartering

bar ter ing

▶ "This looks like a difficult word until we break it into three syllables. See, each syllable has a vowel. When we say each syllable, you can feel your mouth open. Each syllable has one beat."

un der stand ing

trans port ing

sub tract ing

▶ "First, read these long words already broken into syllables. Then read the word fast."

meaningful   smalltime

imperfect   confirming

▶ "Now break these words into syllables, read the syllables, and then read the word."

(See the Additional Supplementary Reading Scope and Sequence in the *Tutor Handbook* for additional titles.)

Book Reading

▶ Read *Samantha*.

ea
leaf

Say the Sounds

▶ "Point to each letter pair. Say the sound."

▶ "The ea vowel team sounds like the letter name e."

ea	ai	oa	oo
	rain	boat	broom

ay	ai	al	oa
hay		salt	

ee	oo	ea	ay
tree	book		

"Write the letter pair that makes the _____ sound."

Choose three or more sounds for spelling.

Word Reading

▶ "Sound these out and say them fast."

Choose six difficult words.

"Now you spell _____."

"Underline the letter pair(s) or word part(s) you know in the word."

"Read the word."

team	dealer	lean
sealed	treated	yeast
heated	painter	slightly
meanest	tray	trailer
beans	train	roast

kind	find

no	kind	are
who	any	eyes
kind	go	find
their	aren't	eyes
any	their	don't

▶ "This word is _____."

"You read it."

"Point and spell."

"What word?"

"Read each word."

Choose four difficult words for student to spell and read.

▶ "Read these sentences. Point to each word."

Did anyone stay up late to see the comet? A comet looks like a falling star. Some kinds of comets aren't hard to find in the sky. We stayed up very late. We saw five or six bright shooting stars.

▶ "Long words are made of syllables and are easy to read when we break them up into smaller chunks."

▶ "We can find the syllables by looking for and hearing the vowels."

different
dif fer ent

▶ "This looks like a difficult word until we break it into three syllables. See, each syllable has a vowel. When we say each syllable, you can feel your mouth open. Each syllable has one beat."

tea spoon ful

un pack ing

dis play ing

▶ "First, read these long words already broken into syllables. Then read the word fast."

underground   seacoast

leadership   layering

▶ "Now break these words into syllables, read the syllables, and then read the word."

(See the Additional Supplementary Reading Scope and Sequence in the *Tutor Handbook* for additional titles.)

Book Reading

▶ Read *Samantha*.

Mastery Test 7

Use with Mastery Test 7—Tester Recording Sheet (see *Tutor Handbook*).

Sounds

▶ "Point to each letter pair and say the sound."

ay	oo	oa
oo	ai	ea
al	ow	ew
ue	ou	er

(Provide student with Mastery Test 7—Student Recording Sheet found in *Tutor Handbook*.)

"Write the letters that make the _____ sound."

Word Reading

▶ "Sound these words out, then read them fast."

playing	book	loafing
room	stray	roasted
sailing	tooth	dealer
brain	failed	cartoons
treats	layer	float

(Provide student with Mastery Test 7—Student Recording Sheet found in *Tutor Handbook*.)

Spelling

"I say the word, and you write the word."

don't their find we've

who eyes from are

no kind aren't so

go we'll

**Sight Word
Reading**

▶ "Read these words."

ea
leaf

ai	ay	ea	ee
rain	hay		tree

oa	ou	oo	ee
boat	cloud	broom	

ea	oo	ai	ea
	book		

Say the Sounds

▶ "Point to each letter pair. Say the sound."

▶ "Remember, the <u>ea</u> vowel team sounds like the letter name <u>e</u>."

"Write the letter pair that makes the _____ sound."

Choose three or more sounds for spelling.

Word Reading

▶ "Sound these out and say them fast."

Choose six difficult words.

"Now you spell _____."

"Underline the letter pair(s) or word part(s) you know in the word."

"Read the word."

heated	nailing	meets
treats	beater	float
reads	street	cheat
healing	green	lighter
layer	wheat	deep

both

▶ "This word is _____."

"You read it."

"Point and spell."

"What word?"

"Read each word."

aren't	both	kind
are	eyes	go
who	their	so
from	both	find
eyes	are	both

Choose four difficult words for student to spell and read.

▶ "Read these sentences. Point to each word."

Both of those trees are bare. They don't have a leaf on them. The wind blew them all down. So now we have to rake them up and clean up our yard.

▶ "Long words are made of syllables and are easy to read when we break them up into smaller chunks."

▶ "We can find the syllables by looking for and hearing the vowels."

---

pickpockets

pick pock ets

▶ "This looks like a difficult word until we break it into three syllables. See, each syllable has a vowel. When we say each syllable, you can feel your mouth open. Each syllable has one beat."

---

grass hop per

out stand ing

sun rise

▶ "First, read these long words already broken into syllables. Then read the word fast."

---

lemonade   steamship

seesaw   imperfect

▶ "Now break these words into syllables, read the syllables, and then read the word."

(See the Additional Supplementary Reading Scope and Sequence in the *Tutor Handbook* for additional titles.)

Book Reading

▶ Read *The Class Trip*.

ir
bird

Say the Sounds

▶ "Point to each letter pair. Say the sound."

▶ "When i̱ is followed by ṟ, the letters say /ir/."

ea	ir	oa	oo
leaf		boat	broom
ir	ea	ee	ou
		tree	cloud
ow	ir	ea	ay
clown			hay

Word Reading

▶ "Sound these out and say them fast."

Choose six difficult words.

"Now you spell _____."

"Underline the letter pair(s) or word part(s) you know in the word."

"Read the word."

fir	birch	peach
stir	owls	mighty
peek	sir	boats
girls	birth	first
dirt	flight	steaming

where

both	where	many
eyes	are	go
both	who	where
find	both	from
their	so	we'll

I don't know where my sneakers are. They might be under my bed. They aren't in my locker at school. I don't have any for the basketball game tonight!

▶ "This word is _____."

"You read it."

"Point and spell."

"What word?"

"Read each word."

Choose four difficult words for student to spell and read.

▶ "Read these sentences. Point to each word."

off   fill   pass

fizz   fluff   smell

mess   buzz   stiff

dull   hiss   jazz

puff   still   grass

(See the Additional Supplementary Reading Scope and Sequence in the *Tutor Handbook* for additional titles.)

NEW! Double Consonants

▶ "When the letters f, s, l, or z come after a short vowel in a one-syllable word, they are usually doubled."

▶ "Read these words."

Choose six words for student to spell and read.

"Now you spell _____."

"Listen to the vowel sound and spell these words."

glass	maze
fail	pill
pail	coal
huff	leaf

▶ *For each word:*

"Why is/isn't there a double _____?"

"What is the vowel sound?"

Book Reading

▶ Read *The Class Trip*.

ir
bird

ea	**ow**	**ai**	**ir**
leaf	clown	rain	
ou	**ir**	**er**	**ea**
cloud		fern	
ee	**ow**	**oo**	**ue**
tree		book	blue

stir	cloudy	whirl
shampoo	tighten	birds
growl	steaming	shirt
sneak	coffee	thirsty
hooks	canteen	squirm

aren't	where	find
who	were	where
eyes	want	both
don't	from	where
are	any	all

Choose four difficult words for student to spell and read.

▶ "Read these sentences. Point to each word."

Do you know where my sneakers are? Both of them were under the couch. My pet dog, Skippy, got them out of my backpack. Skippy hid them. I found them just in time to get to the game.

puff	doll	moss
staff	smell	fuss
sniff	grill	class
muff	fell	press
cliff	thrill	dress

(See the Additional Supplementary Reading Scope and Sequence in the *Tutor Handbook* for additional titles.)

Double Consonants

► "When the letters f, s, l, or z come after a short vowel in a one-syllable word, they are usually doubled."

► "Read these words."

Choose six words for student to spell and read.

"Now you spell ____."

"Listen to the vowel sound and spell these words."

goal	mill
beef	scuff
mail	cliff
tool	spill

► *For each word:*

"Why is/isn't there a double ____?"

"What is the vowel sound?"

Book Reading

► Read *The Game*.

Say the Sounds

▶ "Point to each letter pair. Say the sound."

oa boat	**ir** bird	**ea** leaf	**ai** rain
ay hay	**oo** book	**al** salt	**ar** car
ew scr<u>ew</u>	**ee** tree	**er** fern	**qu** queen
ch cherry	**ue** blue	**wh** whale	**sh** sheep
ir	**ar**	**ay**	**ai**
qu	**wh**	**ue**	**oa**

"Write the letter pair that makes the _____ sound."

Choose three or more sounds for spelling.

coasters   shine   march

while   hunter   trash

cartoons   drew   walrus

mighty   player   skirt

choke   booklet   toad

Word Reading

▶ "Sound these out and say them fast."

Choose six difficult words.

"Now you spell _____."

"Underline the letter pair(s) or word part(s) you know in the word."

"Read the word."

▶ "Read each word."

where	any	both
says	are	any
very	where	kind
eyes	their	are
live	knew	aren't

Choose four difficult words for student to spell and read.

▶ "Read these sentences. Point to each word."

Now that I know how to read, I find all kinds of good books. In my house I have counted thirty books that aren't hard. I can read them. My sister says I'm a very good reader, and she's right!

fuzz	whiff	quill
press	cuff	well
fuss	sniff	spell
buzz	miss	spill
jazz	Jeff	chill

Double Consonants

▶ "When the letters f, s, l, or z come after a short vowel in a one-syllable word, they are usually doubled."

▶ "Read these words."

"Listen to the vowel sound and spell these words."

pose	fluff
pass	male
maze	less
loaf	Jeff

▶ *For each word:*

"Why is/isn't there a double _____?"

"What is the vowel sound?"

(See the Additional Supplementary Reading Scope and Sequence in the *Tutor Handbook* for additional titles.)

Book Reading

▶ Read *The Game*.

kn

knife

NEW!
Letter Pairs
Say the Sounds

▶ "Point to each letter pair. Say the underlined pair first. Then read the word."

▶ "The <u>k</u> is silent in this letter pair."

<u>kn</u>ife	<u>kn</u>ee	<u>kn</u>ot
<u>kn</u>elt	<u>kn</u>it	<u>kn</u>eel
<u>kn</u>ock	<u>kn</u>ight	<u>kn</u>ob

Choose three words for student to write and read.

Word Reading

▶ "Sound these out and say them fast."

knead	thirsty	knits
kicked	nightly	marsh
stout	doorknob	stew
penknife	beast	knotty
crook	saint	scarf

Choose six difficult words.

"Now you spell _____."

"Underline the letter pair(s) or word part(s) you know in the word."

"Read the word."

have   where   any

are   their   both

very   eyes   says

who   where   from

find   no   where

▶ "Read each word."

Choose four difficult words for student to spell and read.

▶ "Read these sentences. Point to each word."

We found both of the trees. They were very green. One is an elm tree. One is an oak tree. I drew the shapes of the leaves in my art class.

(See the Additional Supplementary Reading Scope and Sequence in the *Tutor Handbook* for additional titles.)

Book Reading

▶ Read *Mice and Beans.*

wr
wreck

<u>wr</u>ap	<u>wr</u>ist	<u>kn</u>ife
<u>kn</u>ot	<u>wr</u>ite	<u>wr</u>eath
<u>wr</u>ote	<u>kn</u>it	<u>wr</u>ench

chart rooster started

unwrap write east

kneecap   shipwreck

twisted   knapsack

shark waist chirps

Letter Pairs
Say the Sounds

▶ "Point to each
letter pair. Say the
underlined pair first.
Then read
the word."

▶ "The <u>w</u> is silent in this
letter pair."

*Choose three words
for student to write
and read.*

Word Reading

▶ "Sound these out and
say them fast."

*Choose six difficult
words.*

"Now you spell
_____."

"Underline the letter
pair(s) or word part(s)
you know in the word."

"Read the word."

walk	talk

have	walk	where
both	talk	any
are	very	who
where	their	talk

I will write an e-mail. I will invite all the girls who live near me to a party. They will come to my house. We will walk by the lake and talk late into the night. We have all kinds of jokes to tell.

(See the Additional Supplementary Reading Scope and Sequence in the *Tutor Handbook* for additional titles.)

▶ "This word is _____."

"You read it."

"Point and spell."

"What word?"

"Read each word."

Choose four difficult words for student to spell and read.

▶ "Read these sentences. Point to each word."

Book Reading

▶ Read *Mice and Beans.*

<u>wr</u>eck   <u>kn</u>eel   <u>wr</u>ote

<u>wr</u>ap   <u>kn</u>ight   <u>wr</u>ing

<u>kn</u>ead   <u>wr</u>eath   <u>kn</u>ife

<u>kn</u>itting   <u>kn</u>otted

**Letter Pairs
Say the Sounds**

▶ "Point to each letter pair. Say the underlined pair first. Then read the word."

▶ "The <u>w</u> is silent in the letter pair <u>wr</u>."

▶ "The <u>k</u> is silent in the letter pair <u>kn</u>."

Choose three words for student to write and read.

knock   swirl   wrench

thirst   knees   chirped

wrist   cheat   wrench

smirk   croak   kneepad

third   snail   wrong

Word Reading

▶ "Sound these out and say them fast."

Choose six difficult words.

"Now you spell
_____."

"Underline the letter pair(s) or word part(s) you know in the word."

"Read the word."

where	walk	who
both	talk	any
are	their	have
many	head	don't
find	for	kind

Choose four difficult words for student to spell and read.

▶ "Read these sentences. Point to each word."

Don't wrap the gift yet. I want to write a note and insert it into the box. He will find it when he unwraps the gift.

(See the Additional Supplementary Reading Scope and Sequence in the *Tutor Handbook* for additional titles.)

Book Reading

▶ Read *Mice and Beans.*

-ng

swi<u>ng</u>

Letter Pairs
Say the Sounds

▶ "Point to each letter pair. Say the underlined pair first. Then read the word."

▶ "The letter pair <u>ng</u> makes **one** sound. It is a single nasal sound you make at the back of your mouth, /ng/."

si<u>ng</u>   lo<u>ng</u>   ri<u>ng</u>

so<u>ng</u>   ba<u>ng</u>i<u>ng</u>   fa<u>ng</u>s

ha<u>ng</u>i<u>ng</u>   ga<u>ng</u>   swi<u>ng</u>

lu<u>ng</u>s   di<u>ng</u>   bri<u>ng</u>

cla<u>ng</u>i<u>ng</u>   thi<u>ng</u>s   stri<u>ng</u>y

Choose three words for student to write and read.

chained	showers	reaching
mouth	string	slouching
twirl	slang	artist
wrong	brightly	slingshot
sung	freeway	fainted

Word Reading

▶ "Sound these out and say them fast."

Choose six difficult words.

"Now you spell _____."

"Underline the letter pair(s) or word part(s) you know in the word."

"Read the word."

because

walk	live	because
where	because	both
are	any	who
kind	because	says
where	talk	very

Sight Words

▶ "This word is _____."

"You read it."

"Point and spell."

"What word?"

"Read each word."

Choose four difficult words for student to spell and read.

I am his good buddy because both of us like to talk and fish. We go fishing where the stream is fast. The fish like to hide under the rocks to stay cool.

▶ "Read these sentences. Point to each word."

(See the Additional Supplementary Reading Scope and Sequence in the *Tutor Handbook* for additional titles.)

Book Reading

▶ Read *Joe's Toe*.

-ng

swing

ringing	wings	long
strong	hanger	sang
thing	swing	stung

falling	archer	daylight
shirts	trailing	reached
pleated	slightly	loudest
sleeping	gaining	brings
rounded	wrong	clanging

Letter Pairs
Say the Sounds

▶ "Point to each letter pair. Say the underlined pair first. Then read the word."

▶ "Remember, the letter pair ng makes **one** sound, /ng/."

Choose three words for student to write and read.

Word Reading

▶ "Sound these out and say them fast."

Choose six difficult words.

"Now you spell _____."

"Underline the letter pair(s) or word part(s) you know in the word."

"Read the word."

put

because	talk	put
where	live	because
both	put	where
walk	find	put

► "This word is _____."

"You read it."

"Point and spell."

"What word?"

"Read each word."

Choose four difficult words for student to spell and read.

My teacher asked me to put my books in my cubby. I had to make room for them, because I had put a visiting girl's books in there, too. The girl was visiting my class because she might come to my school next year.

► "Read these sentences. Point to each word."

(See the Additional Supplementary Reading Scope and Sequence in the *Tutor Handbook* for additional titles.)

Book Reading

► Read *Joe's Toe.*

-nk

drink

pi<u>nk</u>	sti<u>nk</u>	ho<u>nk</u>
ju<u>nk</u>	ta<u>nk</u>er	i<u>nk</u>
ya<u>nk</u>ed	mi<u>nk</u>	si<u>nk</u>ing

staying	stinking	spool
trunk	blink	hunk
thanks	shrunk	springs
charcoal	Spain	coach
squirt	tattoo	third

Letter Pairs
Say the Sounds

▶ "Point to each letter pair. Say the underlined pair first. Then read the word."

▶ "The letter pair <u>nk</u> makes **two** sounds, /nk/. The <u>n</u> makes the /ng/ sound and the <u>k</u> makes the /k/ sound."

Choose three words for student to write and read.

Word Reading

▶ "Sound these out and say them fast."

Choose six difficult words.

"Now you spell _____."

"Underline the letter pair(s) or word part(s) you know in the word."

"Read the word."

your	four

where	live	four
because	kind	put
your	there	have
because	find	your

Sight Words

▶ "This word is _____."

"You read it."

"Point and spell."

"What word?"

"Read each word."

Choose four difficult words for student to spell and read.

Your scout leader knows a lot about mushrooms. He knows where to find them and what kinds are safe to eat. On a walk with him, we found four rare ones.

▶ "Read these sentences. Point to each word."

(See the Additional Supplementary Reading Scope and Sequence in the *Tutor Handbook* for additional titles.)

Book Reading

▶ Read *The Picnic*.

Mastery Test 8

Use with Mastery Test—Tester Recording Sheet (see *Tutor Handbook*).

ir   kn   wr

−ng   −nk

Sounds

▶ "Point to each letter or letter pair and say the sound."

"Write the letters that make the _____ sound."

(Provide student with Mastery Test 8—Student Recording Sheet found in *Tutor Handbook*.)

birthday	knee	hanging
stringy	finger	honk
knight	tanker	slingshot
yanked	knife	wrench
wreath	thirsty	junk

Word Reading

▶ "Sound these words out, then read them fast."

(Provide student with Mastery Test 8—Student Recording Sheet found in *Tutor Handbook*.)

Spelling

"I say the word, and you write the word."

your	where	talk	because
walk	put	four	both

Sight Word Reading

▶ "Read these words."

spring   <u>wr</u>ist   <u>wr</u>ench

<u>kn</u>itted   bli<u>nk</u>   sa<u>ng</u>

<u>wr</u>eck   bo<u>nk</u>   <u>kn</u>ock

pla<u>nk</u>   thi<u>nk</u>   <u>wr</u>apper

Letter Pairs
Say the Sounds

▶ "Point to each letter pair. Say the underlined pair first. Then read the word."

▶ "There are silent letters in some of these pairs."

Choose three words for student to write and read.

---

clank   clink   write

knots   thirst   chirps

spray   wrong   stream

headstrong   meantime

tanker   nightmare   sour

Word Reading

▶ "Sound these out and say them fast."

Choose six difficult words.

"Now you spell _____."

"Underline the letter pair(s) or word part(s) you know in the word."

"Read the word."

your	put	four
because	walk	where
both	talk	kind
aren't	your	their
we've	four	put

Last summer I took a four mile walk with my sister. We went to find a fire lookout. When we got there, we found some old bricks and nails. They were all that was left of the fire lookout.

(See the Additional Supplementary Reading Scope and Sequence in the *Tutor Handbook* for additional titles.)

C
(soft)

circle

i<u>c</u>e	<u>c</u>ent	<u>c</u>ircus
<u>c</u>enter	<u>c</u>ell	<u>c</u>inder
pla<u>c</u>e	<u>c</u>ellar	fa<u>c</u>e
pen<u>c</u>il	Pa<u>c</u>ific	fan<u>c</u>y

sticking	quicker	pencil
honk	knickers	bringing
painting	ice cream	rocket
flashlight	acid	pounding
stinger	offside	crosswalk

Say the Sounds

▶ "Say the underlined letter first. Then read the word."

▶ "The letter <u>c</u> usually makes the /s/ sound when it is followed by an <u>e</u>, <u>i</u>, or <u>y</u>."

Choose three words for student to write and read.

Word Reading

▶ "Sound these out and say them fast."

Choose six difficult words.

"Now you spell _____."

"Underline the letter pair(s) or word part(s) you know in the word."

"Read the word."

do

because	kind	do
talk	says	there
find	do	walk
do	because	kind
four	put	your

What do you do when you find something that someone has lost at school? You put it in the lost and found, because then someone might find it there.

(See the Additional Supplementary Reading Scope and Sequence in the *Tutor Handbook* for additional titles.)

▶ "This word is _____."

"You read it."

"Point and spell."

"What word?"

"Read each word."

Choose four difficult words for student to spell and read.

▶ "Read these sentences. Point to each word."

Book Reading

▶ Read *The Picnic*.

g
(soft)

<u>g</u>iraffe

Say the Sounds

▶ "Say the underlined letter first. Then read the word."

▶ "The letter <u>g</u> usually makes the /j/ sound when it is followed by an <u>e</u>, <u>i</u>, or <u>y</u>."

<u>g</u>erm	pa<u>g</u>e	a<u>g</u>e
hu<u>g</u>e	<u>g</u>em	<u>g</u>ently
<u>g</u>inger	<u>g</u>elatin	ra<u>g</u>e
lar<u>g</u>e	ener<u>g</u>y	<u>g</u>ym

Choose three words for student to write and read.

Word Reading

▶ "Sound these out and say them fast."

staff	face	ginger
slice	stiffer	rocks
banker	stage	energy
checkbook		nightgown
playground		gerbil

Choose six difficult words.

"Now you spell _____."

"Underline the letter pair(s) or word part(s) you know in the word."

"Read the word."

move

do	because	kind
live	move	find
your	talk	put
move	where	have

▶ "This word is _____."

"You read it."

"Point and spell."

"What word?"

"Read each word."

Choose four difficult words for student to spell and read.

▶ "Read these sentences. Point to each word."

Next year we will move because we need a bigger place to live. The move will be good. We will have more room to put our things. But I will miss talking to my very good pals very much.

(See the Additional Supplementary Reading Scope and Sequence in the *Tutor Handbook* for additional titles.)

Book Reading

▶ Read *Bed Bugs*.

germ   cell   fancy

page   place   gym

center   rice   gem

cent   huge   lace

---

fence   bumper   knocking

ace   wrong   thinks

germ   hug   huge

rice   rich   race

lack   lace   place

move	do	because
kind	live	your
move	talk	put
where	have	move
because	live	kind

Choose four difficult words for student to spell and read.

▶ "Read these sentences. Point to each word."

Cindy helped me move a huge pile of dirt from the driveway. The dirt was for our garden. We moved the dirt over by the fence. After we dig holes for the plants, we will put the dirt in the garden.

(See the Additional Supplementary Reading Scope and Sequence in the *Tutor Handbook* for additional titles.)

Book Reading

▶ Read *Bed Bugs*.

Say the Sounds

▶ "Say the underlined letter first. Then read the word."

▶ "Remember, when c or g are followed by e, i, or y, they are soft."

Choose three words for student to write and read.

g̲ym   C̲indy   pric̲e

rag̲e   spic̲e   c̲entral

energ̲y   slic̲e   g̲erbil

c̲ell   pag̲e   fanc̲y

Word Reading

▶ "Sound these out and say them fast."

Choose six difficult words.

"Now you spell _____."

"Underline the letter pair(s) or word part(s) you know in the word."

"Read the word."

mice   might   whirling

face   center   canter

page   pigpen   slice

slicker   fence   higher

friend

friend	do	four
your	put	because
friend	walk	where
both	kind	move
eyes	from	aren't

▶ "This word is _____."

"You read it."

"Point and spell."

"What word?"

"Read each word."

Choose four difficult words for student to spell and read.

My class had a talent show. We had to move the desks to make room for a stage. I can juggle four balls, so that's what I did.

▶ "Read these sentences. Point to each word."

(See the Additional Supplementary Reading Scope and Sequence in the *Tutor Handbook* for additional titles.)

Book Reading

▶ Read *The King, Part I.*

or
fork

Say the Sounds

▶ "Say the underlined pair first. Then read the word."

▶ "When o is followed by r, the letters say /or/."

order	for	sport
orbit	sorts	normal
border	forest	morning
pork	forbid	cork

Choose three words for student to write and read.

Word Reading

▶ "Sound these out and say them fast."

stork	hang	shortest
steaming	corn	shock
stem	forty	lucky
sorting	story	sticker
popcorn	hornpipe	foghorn

Choose six difficult words.

"Now you spell _____."

"Underline the letter pair(s) or word part(s) you know in the word."

"Read the word."

sure

friend	kind	your
put	sure	because
says	find	where
don't	their	friend
sure	are	who

"Don't move," he said to his dad. "I'm sure this is where I saw the deer's footprints on the trail." He was sure because he marked the place with a large rock.

(See the Additional Supplementary Reading Scope and Sequence in the *Tutor Handbook* for additional titles.)

Book Reading

▶ Read *The King, Part I.*

or

f<u>or</u>k

gl<u>or</u>y	sh<u>or</u>ter	d<u>or</u>mit<u>or</u>y
fl<u>or</u>ist	m<u>or</u>ning	st<u>or</u>y
c<u>or</u>ner	<u>or</u>dering	h<u>or</u>n
h<u>or</u>net	b<u>or</u>ing	st<u>or</u>k

sticky	snoring	strike
squirt	clay	clang
beans	roasted	shouting
forks	shorthand	streaky
seaport	bricks	cornhusk

Say the Sounds

▶ "Say the underlined pair first. Then read the word."

▶ "Remember, when <u>o</u> is followed by <u>r</u>, the letters say /or/."

Choose three words for student to write and read.

Word Reading

▶ "Sound these out and say them fast."

Choose six difficult words.

"Now you spell _____."

"Underline the letter pair(s) or word part(s) you know in the word."

"Read the word."

little

move	do	little
put	where	friend
kind	any	little
friend	little	because
are	move	sure

Sight Words

▶ "This word is _____."

"You read it."

"Point and spell."

"What word?"

"Read each word."

Choose four difficult words for student to spell and read.

We rode our bikes up and down the hill. Little by little we got very tired. Then we put our packs on and rode home for lunch. We sure were hungry!

▶ "Read these sentences. Point to each word."

(See the Additional Supplementary Reading Scope and Sequence in the *Tutor Handbook* for additional titles.)

Book Reading

▶ Read *The King, Part II.*

aw

saw

Say the Sounds

▶ "Say the underlined pair first. Then read the word."

▶ "When <u>a</u> is followed by <u>w</u>, the letters say /aw/."

l<u>aw</u>n	<u>aw</u>ful	str<u>aw</u>
cl<u>aw</u>	cr<u>aw</u>l	g<u>aw</u>k
<u>aw</u>kward	p<u>aw</u>s	sh<u>aw</u>l
r<u>aw</u>	sees<u>aw</u>	outl<u>aw</u>

Choose three words for student to write and read.

glory	crawling	checkers
playing	jaws	cheating
sprayer	wheat	gray
jawbone	meaty	flickers
glide	drawing	jigsaw

Word Reading

▶ "Sound these out and say them fast."

Choose six difficult words.

"Now you spell _____."

"Underline the letter pair(s) or word part(s) you know in the word."

"Read the word."

shiny

little	move	shiny
do	walk	sure
put	because	do
friend	move	shiny
little	shiny	put

▶ "This word is _____."

"You read it."

"Point and spell."

"What word?"

"Read each word."

Choose four difficult words for student to spell and read.

Here is the game: Take a walk around your house and find four shiny things. They might be shiny dimes or shiny forks or anything shiny. The first one to find four shiny objects wins!

▶ "Read these sentences. Point to each word."

(See the Additional Supplementary Reading Scope and Sequence in the *Tutor Handbook* for additional titles.)

Book Reading

▶ Read *The King, Part II.*

aw

s<u>aw</u>

Say the Sounds

▶ "Say the underlined pair first. Then read the word."

▶ "When <u>a</u> is followed by <u>w</u>, the letters say /aw/."

p<u>aw</u>s	br<u>aw</u>ny	cl<u>aw</u>
s<u>aw</u>mill	y<u>aw</u>ning	s<u>aw</u>
h<u>aw</u>k	sees<u>aw</u>	d<u>aw</u>n
cr<u>aw</u>ling	r<u>aw</u>	outl<u>aw</u>

Choose three words for student to write and read.

Word Reading

▶ "Sound these out and say them fast."

short	awful	yucky
forty	players	sawmill
port	Sunday	pork
north	torn	organ
plywood		jaywalk
	mainstream	

Choose six difficult words.

"Now you spell _____."

"Underline the letter pair(s) or word part(s) you know in the word."

"Read the word."

again

shiny	again	walk
move	do	kind
put	because	little
find	walk	friend
move	again	shiny

▶ "This word is _____."

"You read it."

"Point and spell."

"What word?"

"Read each word."

Choose four difficult words for student to spell and read.

▶ "Read these sentences. Point to each word."

We walked around the house again to find four more shiny things. They were for your sister, who was crying. She smiled again when she saw the shiny little nickels, dimes, and quarters.

▶ "We can read long words by breaking them up into smaller chunks."

sat is fac tor y

satisfactory

▶ "I'll show you."

▶ "You read the parts, then read the word."

At lan tic

im per fect

saw dust

▶ "First read these long words already broken into syllables. Then read the word fast."

janitor   togetherness

powerful   establish

▶ "Now break these words into syllables, read the syllables, and then read the word."

(See the Additional Supplementary Reading Scope and Sequence in the *Tutor Handbook* for additional titles.)

Book Reading

▶ Read *The Train*.

sku<u>nk</u>   dr<u>aw</u>ing   th<u>or</u>n

<u>f</u>orest   str<u>aw</u>   <u>wr</u>ong

pa<u>g</u>e   <u>kn</u>eel   <u>kn</u>ob

<u>wr</u>ap   <u>g</u>erm   <u>i</u>ce cream

<u>c</u>igar   ta<u>nk</u>er   <u>kn</u>it

<u>wr</u>ote   pen<u>c</u>il   ju<u>nk</u>

circus   junk   written

pocket   straw   gently

shipwreck   drew   knockout

drain   stuffy   toasts

banker   shouted   center

Say the Sounds

▶ "Say the underlined letter or letter pair first. Then read the word."

Choose three words for student to write and read.

Word Reading

▶ "Sound these out and say them fast."

Choose six difficult words.

"Now you spell _____."

"Underline the letter pair(s) or word part(s) you know in the word."

"Read the word."

Lessons **307**   Sound Partners

Sight Words

▶ "Read each word."

little	walk	again
any	want	who
shiny	where	your
friend	are	over
again	because	find

Choose four difficult words for student to spell and read.

▶ "Read these sentences. Point to each word."

After my dad and I had lunch, we walked over to the park to play baseball. We like to play baseball there because we have lots of space. Last year when we played baseball on our sidewalk, a man yelled at us for hitting his shiny car with our ball.

▶ "We can read long words by breaking them up into smaller chunks."

▶ "I'll show you."

▶ "You read the parts, then read the word."

dis in te grate

disintegrate

▶ "First read these long words already broken into syllables. Then read the word fast."

per form ing

sweet en ing

un der stand

▶ "Now break these words into syllables, read the syllables, and then read the word."

entertainment　　splendidly

excavate　　archery

(See the Additional Supplementary Reading Scope and Sequence in the *Tutor Handbook* for additional titles.)

Book Reading

▶ Read *The Train*.

Mastery Test 9

Use with Mastery Test 9—Tester Recording Sheet (see *Tutor Handbook*).

Sounds

- ▶ "Point to each letter or letter pair and say the sound."

c g or

aw er ir

- ▶ "Say the <u>soft</u> sounds for the <u>c</u> and <u>g</u>."

· ·

(Provide student with Mastery Test 9—Student Recording Sheet found in *Tutor Handbook*.)

"Write the letter(s) that makes the _____ sound."

Word Reading

- ▶ "Sound these words out, then read them fast."

cinder	germ	forbid
morning	crawling	age
face	pencil	sorting
straw	energy	hawk
paws	circus	cent

Spelling

(Provide student with Mastery Test 9—Student Recording Sheet found in *Tutor Handbook*.)

"I say the word, and you write the word."

Sight Word Reading

- ▶ "Read these words."

do move friend sure

little shiny again

-le

candle

▶ "Say the underlined pair first. Then read the word."

▶ "The letter pair le usually comes at the end of a word, and the e is silent."

simple	buckle	ankle
angle	dribble	tickle
shuffle	gentle	circle

Choose three words for student to write and read.

Word Reading

▶ "Sound these out and say them fast."

corks	fangs	drawing
stork	thimble	pluck
thorny	little	crinkle
stumble	feast	singer
cricket	jacket	dimple

Choose six difficult words.

"Now you spell _____."

"Underline the letter pair(s) or word part(s) you know in the word."

"Read the word."

brother	other	mother

walk	little	again
other	brother	move
little	mother	do
because	shiny	again
brother	another	mother

Sight Words

▶ "This word is _____."

"You read it."

"Point and spell."

"What word?"

"Read each word."

Choose four difficult words for student to spell and read.

▶ "Read these sentences. Point to each word."

My mother and my big brother will walk to the store. I want shiny candy but my mother will get other things like peaches, meat, and milk. She might bring home some ice cream if they walk fast so it can't melt.

▶ "We can read long words by breaking them up into smaller chunks."

com mand ment

commandment

▶ "I'll show you."

▶ "You read the parts, then read the word."

ram shack le

mean ing less

mis un der stand ing

▶ "First read these long words already broken into syllables. Then read the word fast."

underneath   outstanding

overlook   confident

▶ "Now break these words into syllables, read the syllables, and then read the word."

(See the Additional Supplementary Reading Scope and Sequence in the *Tutor Handbook* for additional titles.)

Book Reading

▶ Read *The Train*.

be-	de-	pre-	re-
<u>be</u>gin	<u>de</u>tect	<u>pre</u>tend	<u>re</u>turn

Say the Sounds

▶ "Say the underlined prefix at the beginning of the word first. Then read the word."

▶ "Prefixes are little word parts at the beginning of a word."

<u>b</u>egin	<u>r</u>eturn	<u>d</u>etect
<u>pr</u>etend	<u>be</u>long	<u>r</u>epay
<u>pr</u>event	<u>re</u>tell	<u>de</u>fend

Choose three words for student to write and read.

Word Reading

▶ "Sound these out and say them fast."

remote	below	decay
border	detach	settle
beside	began	request
portray	reply	between
gently	delight	predict

Choose six difficult words.

"Now you spell
_____."

"Underline the letter pair(s) or word part(s) you know in the word."

"Read the word."

could	should	would
couldn't	shouldn't	wouldn't

▶ "This word is _____."

"You read it."

"Point and spell."

"What word?"

sure	again	would
could	should	little
walk	would	again
any	because	wouldn't
shouldn't	find	do

▶ "Couldn't is a short way to say could not. Shouldn't is a short way to say should not. Wouldn't is a short way to say would not. This mark (') is called an apostrophe. We call these words contractions."

"Read each word."

Choose four difficult words for student to spell and read.

▶ "Read these sentences. Point to each word."

Would you go camping again if you could? I would, because we had a terrific trip. It never rained, and we all got along with each other. We should make plans to go again soon, shouldn't we?

▶ "We can read long words by breaking them up into smaller chunks."

▶ "I'll show you."

▶ "You read the parts, then read the word."

re place ment

replacement

▶ "First read these long words already broken into syllables. Then read the word fast."

be long ing

de mol ish

un thank ful

▶ "Now break these words into syllables, read the syllables, and then read the word."

department   prevented

pretending   memory

(See the Additional Supplementary Reading Scope and Sequence in the *Tutor Handbook* for additional titles.)

Book Reading

▶ Read *Chickens*.

-tion
action

-sion
version

-tion	-sion
ac**tion**	frac**tion**
direc**tion**	man**sion**
ten**sion**	sec**tion**
elec**tion**	fric**tion**
subtrac**tion**	suc**tion**
mis**sion**	vi**sion**

Say the Sounds

▶ "Suffixes are little word parts at the end of a word. Both of these suffixes sound the same, /shun/."

▶ "Say the underlined suffix at the end of the word first. Then read the word."

Choose three words for student to write and read.

short	junction	predict
dribble	babble	buckle
helicopter	session	chuckle
fly	direction	traction
relate	hawks	demand

Word Reading

▶ "Sound these out and say them fast."

Choose six difficult words.

"Now you spell _____."

"Underline the letter pair(s) or word part(s) you know in the word."

"Read the word."

busy

other	busy	again
little	mother	walk
busy	move	would
shouldn't	do	sure
brother	shiny	friend

Lesson 93 cont'd

Sight Words

▶ "This word is _____."

"You read it."

"Point and spell."

"What word?"

"Read each word."

Choose four difficult words for student to spell and read.

▶ "Read these sentences. Point to each word."

Your little brother can move all by himself now! He keeps busy crawling all over the house. He likes to find shiny things to put in his mouth. We have to be careful now. We are busy keeping the place safe for your brother.

Reading Long Words

▶ "We can read long words by breaking them up into smaller chunks."

in ten tion

intention

▶ "I'll show you."

▶ "You read the parts, then read the word."

in ven tion

sub trac tion

fan tas tic

▶ "First read these long words already broken into syllables. Then read the word fast."

division   permission

prevention   polishing

▶ "Now break these words into syllables, read the syllables, and then read the word."

(See the Additional Supplementary Reading Scope and Sequence in the *Tutor Handbook* for additional titles.)

Book Reading

▶ Read *Chickens*.

Say the Sounds

► "Say the underlined letter or letter pair first. Then read the word."

<u>de</u><u>cis</u>ion   frac<u>tion</u>

vi<u>sion</u>   <u>r</u>etire

<u>pr</u>event   <u>g</u>en<u>tle</u>

<u>kn</u>uck<u>le</u>   <u>d</u>etach

<u>be</u>tray   sec<u>tion</u>

ac<u>tion</u>   men<u>tion</u>

Choose three words for student to write and read.

Word Reading

► "Sound these out and say them fast."

decide   scribble   dribble

trickle   attention   sniffle

recess   crumble   precise

stubble   behave   portion

begin   direction   pretend

Choose six difficult words.

"Now you spell _____."

"Underline the letter pair(s) or word part(s) you know in the word."

"Read the word."

thought	bought

bought	should	shiny
thought	little	again
bought	wouldn't	other
busy	sure	shouldn't
thought	friend	move

▶ "This word is _____."

"You read it."

"Point and spell."

"What word?"

"Read each word."

Choose four difficult words for student to spell and read.

▶ "Read these sentences. Point to each word."

I thought you had bought something to eat. When you do, we can take a walk and eat our lunch by the lake. After a little rest, we can go swimming again.

▶ "We can read long words by breaking them up into smaller chunks."

pre dict ing

predicting

▶ "I'll show you."

▶ "You read the parts, then read the word."

de fend er

re port ed

de ci sion

▶ "First read these long words already broken into syllables. Then read the word fast."

construction   departing

performer   pretending

▶ "Now break these words into syllables, read the syllables, and then read the word."

(See the Additional Supplementary Reading Scope and Sequence in the *Tutor Handbook* for additional titles.)

Book Reading

▶ Read *The Visit*.

ur

turtle

Say the Sounds

▶ "Say the underlined pair first. Then read the word."

▶ "When u is followed by r, the letters say /ur/."

Choose three words for student to write and read.

turn	hurt	church
burst	burn	fur
purr	surf	disturb

Word Reading

▶ "Sound these out and say them fast."

Choose six difficult words.

"Now you spell
_____."

"Underline the letter pair(s) or word part(s) you know in the word."

"Read the word."

blurry	smelling	drifted
yelled	crawl	swelled
torch	sniffle	portion
helps	hurt	horn
gentle	action	simple

tiny

thought	tiny	other
could	couldn't	sure
tiny	bought	busy
again	little	thought
brother	tiny	wouldn't

▶ "This word is _____."

"You read it."

"Point and spell."

"What word?"

"Read each word."

Choose four difficult words for student to spell and read.

▶ "Read these sentences. Point to each word."

My little sister thought she could play drums, but she sounded awful! When she gets bigger, my mother should send her to take drumming lessons.

not	is	will

couldn't   it's   I'll

shouldn't   what's   you'll

wouldn't   she's   we'll

isn't   that's

have	am

can't

didn't   we've   I'm

don't   you've

aren't   haven't

NEW!
Contraction Review

▶ "Contractions are words made up of two or more words. The apostrophe replaces the missing letters."

▶ "First read these contractions we have learned."

▶ "What is the long way of saying each word? For example, <u>couldn't</u> is short for <u>could not</u>."

▶ "What are the missing letters in each contraction?"

Choose four words for student to spell.

Reading Long Words

▶ "We can read long words by breaking them up into smaller chunks."

▶ "I'll show you."

▶ "You read the parts, then read the word."

re turn ing

returning

▶ "First read these long words already broken into syllables. Then read the word fast."

in ter est ed

per mis sion

pop sic le

▶ "Now break these words into syllables, read the syllables, and then read the word."

direction   department

prediction   powerful

(See the Additional Supplementary Reading Scope and Sequence in the *Tutor Handbook* for additional titles.)

Book Reading

▶ Read *The Visit*.

ur
turtle

burp	churn	turning
fur	burned	surfing
hurts	nurse	blurry

purple	shelter	popcorn
smelly	turnips	portion
forest	nursery	turned
further	traction	turtle
circle	invention	hurry

Say the Sounds

▶ "Say the underlined pair first. Then read the word."

▶ "Remember, when u is followed by r, the letters say /ur/."

Choose three words for student to write and read.

Word Reading

▶ "Sound these out and say them fast."

Choose six difficult words.

"Now you spell _____."

"Underline the letter pair(s) or word part(s) you know in the word."

"Read the word."

Lessons **327**
Sound Partners

bought	shiny	shouldn't
other	thought	busy
again	could	move
friend	would	sure
bought	tiny	wouldn't
	brother	

Choose four difficult words for student to spell and read.

▶ "Read these sentences. Point to each word."

My brother wouldn't go to his flute lessons. He said he thought flutes were silly. He was very busy doing other things like playing soccer with his friends and reading about outer space.

▶ "We can read long words by breaking them up into smaller chunks."

sat is fac tion

satisfaction

▶ "I'll show you."

▶ "You read the parts, then read the word."

men tion ed

ar tic le

re quire ment

▶ "First read these long words already broken into syllables. Then read the word fast."

pretender   scramble

disturbing   possible

▶ "Now break these words into syllables, read the syllables, and then read the word."

(See the Additional Supplementary Reading Scope and Sequence in the *Tutor Handbook* for additional titles.)

Book Reading

▶ Read *The Visit*.

ur	–tion	be–	aw
de–	–sion	–le	–nk
kn	ur	pre–	wr
re–	or	–ng	ir

reduction	thorn	throttle
gurgle	vision	wrinkle
awful	returning	gentle
decision	action	hurting
knuckle	belong	reorder
mention	depend	further

Choose six difficult words.

"Now you spell _____."

"Underline the letter pair(s) or word part(s) you know in the word."

"Read the word."

tiny	thought	busy
could	other	would
again	bought	brother
shiny	shouldn't	sure
little	couldn't	mother
move	sure	do

Choose four difficult words for student to spell and read.

▶ "Read these sentences. Point to each word."

My brother has many other interests besides playing the flute! Rather than practice his flute, he would dribble his basketball or kick his soccer ball with his friends. He said he thought he was too busy for flute lessons.

▶ "We can read long
words by breaking
them up into smaller
chunks."

dis turb ing
disturbing

▶ "I'll show you."

▶ "You read the parts,
then read the word."

de tec tion

pre dic tion

thun der storm

▶ "First read these long
words already broken
into syllables. Then
read the word fast."

entertainment   subtraction

impossible   disagreement

▶ "Now break these
words into syllables,
read the syllables, and
then read the word."

(See the Additional Supplementary Reading Scope and Sequence in the *Tutor Handbook*
for additional titles.)

Book Reading

▶ Reread favorite stories!

ey

key

turk<u>ey</u>   mon<u>ey</u>   vall<u>ey</u>

donk<u>ey</u>   hon<u>ey</u>   all<u>ey</u>

hock<u>ey</u>   kidn<u>ey</u>   k<u>ey</u>

---

spurs   barley   torch

spelling   corndog   drove

decoration   further

portion   sweltering

nursing   hockey

Say the Sounds

▶ "Say the underlined pair first. Then read the word."

▶ "When <u>e</u> is followed by <u>y</u>, the letters sound like the letter name <u>e</u>."

Choose three words for student to write and read.

Word Reading

▶ "Sound these out and say them fast."

Choose six difficult words.

"Now you spell _____."

"Underline the letter pair(s) or word part(s) you know in the word."

"Read the word."

toward	cried

bought	cried	busy
cried	toward	again
tiny	thought	move
cried	mother	tiny
toward	wouldn't	friend

Sight Words

▶ "This word is _____."

"You read it."

"Point and spell."

"What word?"

"Read each word."

Choose four difficult words for student to spell and read.

▶ "Read these sentences. Point to each word."

My friend Tanner got a trombone. At first he cried because he couldn't play it. He took lessons and got to be very good. It took hard work, and it was worth it!

▶ "We can read long words by breaking them up into smaller chunks."

▶ "I'll show you."

▶ "You read the parts, then read the word."

ram shack le

ramshackle

▶ "First read these long words already broken into syllables. Then read the word fast."

in struc tion

chip munks

fright en ing

▶ "Now break these words into syllables, read the syllables, and then read the word."

rejection   impossible

returning   chimpanzee

(See the Additional Supplementary Reading Scope and Sequence in the *Tutor Handbook* for additional titles.)

Book Reading

▶ Reread favorite stories!

ey

ke<u>y</u>

mon<u>ey</u>   donk<u>ey</u>   kidn<u>ey</u>

hock<u>ey</u>   all<u>ey</u>   vall<u>ey</u>

turk<u>ey</u>   hon<u>ey</u>   k<u>ey</u>

northerner   forty   monkey

hurdle   reporting   wrinkle

birdcage   sawmill   infection

construction   slurp   awful

demanding   furnish   burner

Say the Sounds

▶ "Say the underlined pair first. Then read the word."

▶ "Remember, when <u>e</u> is followed by <u>y</u>, the letters sound like the letter name <u>e</u>."

Choose three words for student to write and read.

Word Reading

▶ "Sound these out and say them fast."

Choose six difficult words.

"Now you spell
_____."

"Underline the letter pair(s) or word part(s) you know in the word."

"Read the word."

sorry	paper

▶ "This word is _____."

"You read it."

"Point and spell."

"What word?"

"Read each word."

busy	paper	cried
sorry	tiny	wouldn't
bought	cried	paper
toward	thought	sorry
shouldn't	toward	paper

Choose four difficult words for student to spell and read.

▶ "Read these sentences. Point to each word."

We should have bought enough paper for both art projects! I am sorry we ran out of paper toward the end of class, because now I have to go to the art supply store again!

not	is	will

couldn't   it's   I'll

shouldn't   what's   you'll

wouldn't   she's   we'll

isn't   that's

have	am

can't

didn't   we've   I'm

don't   you've

aren't   haven't

Contraction Review

► "Contractions are words made up of two or more words. The apostrophe replaces the missing letters."

► "First read these contractions we have learned."

► "What is the long way of saying each word? For example, <u>couldn't</u> is short for <u>could not</u>."

► "What are the missing letters in each contraction?"

Choose four words for student to spell.

▶ "We can read long words by breaking them up into smaller chunks."

in vis ib le

invisible

▶ "I'll show you."

▶ "You read the parts, then read the word."

cor rec tion

mis con duct

for got ten

▶ "First read these long words already broken into syllables. Then read the word fast."

janitor   collection

volleyball   finishing

▶ "Now break these words into syllables, read the syllables, and then read the word."

(See the Additional Supplementary Reading Scope and Sequence in the *Tutor Handbook* for additional titles.)

Book Reading

▶ Reread favorite stories!

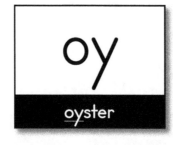

oi
oil

oy
oyster

Say the Sounds

▶ "Say the underlined pair first. Then read the word."

▶ "The oi pair is usually in the middle of the word. The oy pair is usually at the end of a word.""

boil	enjoy	soil
toys	joins	royal
spoiling	soy	moist
coins	pointed	joy
voice	employ	noisy

Choose three words for student to write and read.

Word Reading

▶ "Sound these out and say them fast."

honey	pork	pointed
dirty	foil	ankle
boiler	twinkle	suction
spoiled	sport	soybean
oily	oyster	joint
hockey	cowboy	jungle

Choose six difficult words.

"Now you spell
_____."

"Underline the letter pair(s) or word part(s) you know in the word."

"Read the word."

laugh	beautiful

Sight Words

▶ "This word is _____."

"You read it."

"Point and spell."

"What word?"

"Read each word."

tiny	cried	laugh
sorry	beautiful	paper
thought	laugh	cried
beautiful	couldn't	busy
paper	cried	toward

Choose four difficult words for student to spell and read.

▶ "Read these sentences. Point to each word."

My friends laugh when I tell them the story of my first day of snowboarding. The snow was beautiful. Good thing, because I got snow in my ears, nose, and mouth! I laugh now too when I remember it.

▶ "We can read long words by breaking them up into smaller chunks."

car pen ter

carpenter

▶ "I'll show you."

▶ "You read the parts, then read the word."

at ten tion

un der neath

rat tle snake

▶ "First read these long words already broken into syllables. Then read the word fast."

competition   hamburgers

disrespect   evergreen

▶ "Now break these words into syllables, read the syllables, and then read the word."

(See the Additional Supplementary Reading Scope and Sequence in the *Tutor Handbook* for additional titles.)

Book Reading

▶ Reread favorite stories!

oi

oy

<u>oi</u>l

<u>oy</u>ster

b<u>oi</u>ler	m<u>oi</u>st	<u>oi</u>ly
c<u>oi</u>ns	destr<u>oy</u>	p<u>oi</u>nted
j<u>oi</u>ning	cowb<u>oy</u>	n<u>oi</u>sy
f<u>oi</u>l	br<u>oi</u>l	s<u>oi</u>led
enj<u>oy</u>ing	R<u>oy</u>	d<u>oi</u>ly

turkey	corks	mention
burner	enjoy	spoiled
monkey	honey	employ
jiggle	invention	keys
saddle	direction	soy

Say the Sounds

▶ "Say the underlined pair first. Then read the word."

Choose three words for student to write and read.

Word Reading

▶ "Sound these out and say them fast."

Choose six difficult words.

"Now you spell _____."

"Underline the letter pair(s) or word part(s) you know in the word."

"Read the word."

through	neighbor	

► "This word is _____."

"You read it."

"Point and spell."

"What word?"

"Read each word."

sorry	paper	through
laugh	thought	beautiful
neighbor	through	laugh
bought	neighbor	through
toward	busy	laugh

Choose four difficult words for student to spell and read.

- -

► "Read these sentences. Point to each word."

My neighbor had to crawl through the shrubs to find his newspaper. The dog had hid the newspaper in the dirt. Maybe the dog thought it was a bone. That made me and my brother laugh!

▶ "We can read long words by breaking them up into smaller chunks."

en joy ment
enjoyment

▶ "I'll show you."

▶ "You read the parts, then read the word."

sub scrip tion

con trib ute

Sep tem ber

▶ "First read these long words already broken into syllables. Then read the word fast."

anteater   backpacking

entertainment   disappointed

▶ "Now break these words into syllables, read the syllables, and then read the word."

(See the Additional Supplementary Reading Scope and Sequence in the *Tutor Handbook* for additional titles.)

Book Reading

▶ Read *Poppleton and Friends*, Chapter 1.

b<u>oi</u>led   t<u>ur</u>ning   mon<u>ey</u>

gent<u>le</u>   dribb<u>le</u>   dist<u>ur</u>bs

vall<u>ey</u>   <u>re</u>t<u>ur</u>ning   <u>de</u>c<u>oy</u>

<u>aw</u>nings   sp<u>oi</u>led   tinf<u>oil</u>

enj<u>oy</u>   p<u>oi</u>nter   frac<u>tion</u>

REVIEW
Say the Sounds

▶ "Say the underlined pair first. Then read the word."

Choose three words for student to write and read.

Thursday   thimble   turtle

loyal   morning   keychain

mention   joining   corner

monkey   royalty   crumble

employment   yawning

prevention   embroider

attention   corduroy

Word Reading

▶ "Sound these out and say them fast."

Choose six difficult words.

"Now you spell _____."

"Underline the letter pair(s) or word part(s) you know in the word."

"Read the word."

cookies	eight

sorry	laugh	cookies
through	eight	neighbor
cookies	paper	eight
beautiful	toward	through
friend	eight	cookies

My next door neighbor said I could invite eight friends for a snack. She had baked fresh cookies. My friends and I had helped rake her yard and cut her grass. She wanted to thank us.

news paper man

pre tend ed

trans form er

de struc tion

▶ "You read the parts, then read the word fast."

- -

amusement

programmer

respectful

windowpane

▶ "You read the words by first breaking them into parts."

(See the Additional Supplementary Reading Scope and Sequence in the *Tutor Handbook* for additional titles.)

Book Reading

▶ Read *Poppleton and Friends*, Chapter 2.

OW

bow

b**ow**l	foll**ow**	m**ow**er
owner	wind**ow**	t**ow**
bl**ow**	yell**ow**	fl**ow**
b**ow**ling	borr**ow**	kn**ow**
sn**ow**ball	gr**ow**ing	
b**ow**tie	l**ow**er	

willow	sorted	turtle
monkey	enjoy	spoiling
pursue	towboat	wiggles
prediction	turkey	soybeans
owner	action	lawnmower

Say the Sounds

▶ "Say the underlined pair first. Then read the word."

▶ "The ow pair has **two** sounds: ow as in clown and ow as in bow. When you see a word you don't know, you have to try both to see which one fits."

Choose three words for student to write and read.

Word Reading

▶ "Sound these out and say them fast."

Choose six difficult words.

"Now you spell _____."

"Underline the letter pair(s) or word part(s) you know in the word."

"Read the word."

enough	lion

Sight Words

▶ "This word is _____."

 "You read it."

 "Point and spell."

 "What word?"

 "Read each word."

sorry	eight	enough
lion	laugh	cookies
neighbor	enough	paper
lion	beautiful	enough
sorry	toward	lion

Choose four difficult words for student to spell and read.

▶ "Read these sentences. Point to each word."

If lions are to survive, they need enough land to hunt. If the numbers of lions dwindle, they may become extinct like other animals without enough habitat.

em ploy ment

pre dic tion

sat is fac tion

re main der

fingernail

encounter

remote

brainstorm

▶ "You read the parts,
then read the
word fast."

▶ "You read the words by
first breaking them
into parts."

(See the Additional Supplementary Reading Scope and Sequence in the *Tutor Handbook*
for additional titles.)

Book Reading

▶ Read *Poppleton and
Friends*, Chapter 3.

OW

b<u>ow</u>

kn<u>ow</u>   thr<u>ow</u>ing   sl<u>ow</u>est

l<u>ow</u>er   foll<u>ow</u>   t<u>ow</u>boat

b<u>ow</u>l   gl<u>ow</u>ing

sn<u>ow</u>storm

---

clawing   stripe   sprinkle

money   cowboy   broiler

follow   snowplow   bundle

loyal   honey   inspection

joyful   fraction   informed

Say the Sounds

▶ "Say the underlined pair first. Then read the word."

▶ "Remember, the <u>ow</u> pair has **two** sounds: <u>ow</u> as in <u>clown</u> and <u>ow</u> as in <u>bow</u>. When you see a word you don't know, you have to try both to see which one fits."

Choose three words for student to write and read.

Word Reading

▶ "Sound these out and say them fast."

Choose six difficult words.

"Now you spell
_____."

"Underline the letter pair(s) or word part(s) you know in the word."

"Read the word."

eggs	cherry

enough   eggs   eight

cherry   cried   cookies

eggs   friend   beautiful

cookies   cherry   enough

eight   toward   laugh

Sight Words

▶ "This word is _____."

"You read it."

"Point and spell."

"What word?"

"Read each word."

Choose four difficult words for student to spell and read.

For our picnic we packed:
- eight hard boiled eggs
- sliced <u>whole</u> wheat toast
- sliced turkey meat
- tiny sweet pickles
- little ginger snap cookies
- an eight-inch sour cherry pie

Everyone brought something they really liked. We had enough food to feed the whole neighborhood.

▶ "Read these sentences. Point to each word."

pre scrip tion

frigh ten ing

Ger man y

cell u lar

interruption

pretender

housekeeper

subscription

(See the Additional Supplementary Reading Scope and Sequence in the *Tutor Handbook* for additional titles.)

Lesson 104 cont'd

**REVIEW
Reading Long
Words**

▶ "You read the parts, then read the word fast."

▶ "You read the words by first breaking them into parts."

Book Reading

▶ Reread favorite stories!

Lessons **355**

Sound Partners

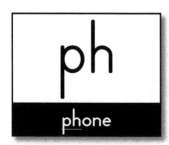

ph
phone

phone	phrase	dolphin
nephew	photo	alphabet
elephant	phantom	telegraph

Say the Sounds

▶ "Say the underlined pair first. Then read the word."

▶ "Ph makes one sound, /f/."

Choose three words for student to write and read.

clues	handle	overdue
partners	coasters	Memphis
noodle	Phil	stowaway
inventions	tickle	cartoons
furnish	telephone	Troy
avenue	thousands	phew

Word Reading

▶ "Sound these out and say them fast."

Choose six difficult words.

"Now you spell
_____."

"Underline the letter pair(s) or word part(s) you know in the word."

"Read the word."

piece	strange

eggs	cherry	strange
lion	enough	eight
piece	strange	neighbor
through	toward	laugh
paper	piece	cried
strange	cookies	piece

Sight Words

▶ "This word is _____."

"You read it."

"Point and spell."

"What word?"

"Read each word."

Choose four difficult words for student to spell and read.

The cherry cake was so good that one piece was not enough. I thought I would ask for another piece, but then there would not be enough for my friends and neighbors.

▶ "Read these sentences. Point to each word."

REVIEW
**Reading Long
Words**

▶ "You read the parts,
then read the
word fast."

de liv er y

can dle stick

in ci dent

nov el ist

▶ "You read the words by
first breaking them
into parts."

perfection

ringleader

define

governor

(See the Additional Supplementary Reading Scope and Sequence in the *Tutor Handbook*
for additional titles.)

Book Reading

▶ Reread favorite stories!

ph

p̲h̲one

p̲h̲ase	grap̲h̲
elep̲h̲ant	nep̲h̲ew
orp̲h̲an	typ̲h̲oon
	alp̲h̲abet

LESSON 106

Say the Sounds

▶ "Say the underlined pair first. Then read the word."

▶ "Ph makes one sound, /f/."

Choose three words for student to write and read.

Sue	sneakers	invention
moody	enjoyment	railroad
starving		Tuesday
charcoal		ankle
photograph		marching

Word Reading

▶ "Sound these out and say them fast."

Choose six difficult words.

"Now you spell
_____."

"Underline the letter pair(s) or word part(s) you know in the word."

"Read the word."

hold	cold

Sight Words

▶ "This word is _____."

"You read it."

"Point and spell."

"What word?"

"Read each word."

piece	through	hold
enough	cold	laugh
friend	cried	eggs
hold	eight	cherry
cookies	through	cold
toward	strange	thought

Choose four difficult words for student to spell and read.

My dad asked me to hold on to the cold drinks. We would all need them when we were through digging up the yard. Our neighbors helped us dig eight holes—enough for the eight cherry trees we bought for Mother's Day. The yard will be beautiful next spring.

▶ "Read these sentences. Point to each word."

in ven tion

con cen trate

de ter gent

Bir ming ham

entertainment

honeymoon

jackhammer

intersection

(See the Additional Supplementary Reading Scope and Sequence in the *Tutor Handbook* for additional titles.)

**REVIEW
Reading Long
Words**

▶ "You read the parts, then read the word fast."

▶ "You read the words by first breaking them into parts."

Book Reading

▶ Reread favorite stories!

Say the Sounds

▶ "Read these letter pairs and word parts."

ph	ey	oi	ow
oy	wr	ur	−sion
kn	be−	aw	−le
−tion	ph	de−	or
ey	ow	oi	pre−

Choose three pairs/ parts for the student to spell.

Word Reading

▶ "Sound these out and say them fast."

elephant	elbow	knife
wreck	reflection	dolphin
expression	spine	hurry
chime	willow	money
alphabet	knock	bowl
straw	bottle	lighter

Choose six difficult words.

"Now you spell _____."

"Underline the letter pair(s) or word part(s) you know in the word."

"Read the word."

Sight Words

▶ "Read each word."

piece	strange	hold
enough	cold	egg
cookies	lion	through
laugh	neighbor	beautiful
sorry	paper	toward
cried	thought	couldn't

Choose four difficult words for student to spell and read.

▶ "Read these sentences. Point to each word."

After we planted the cherry trees, my mother made us lunch. We had boiled eggs and beautiful bowls of corn chowder. Last, we had a big paper bag of peanut butter cookies. We laughed at how sore we were from digging. But the yard looked beautiful.

de struc tion

sen si ble

a part ment

hel i cop ter

- -

presenter

cinnamon

advertise

perfection

(See the Additional Supplementary Reading Scope and Sequence in the *Tutor Handbook* for additional titles.)

▶ "You read the words by first breaking them into parts."

Book Reading

▶ Read student's favorite stories!

ow	ph	oy	or
er	oi	wr	ur
kn	–tion	ph	pre–
ur	re–	–sion	wr
ey	ow	oy	–le

surfer	portion	snuggle
tighten	hockey	mention
ointment	plate	border
throw	knight	graph
annoy	rattle	predict
remark	wreath	blade

Choose six difficult words.

"Now you spell _____."

"Underline the letter pair(s) or word part(s) you know in the word."

"Read the word."

hold	strange	cookies
eight	cold	lion
enough	piece	eggs
through	cherry	neighbor
sorry	toward	laugh
hold	strange	cookies

Choose four difficult words for student to spell and read.

▶ "Read these sentences. Point to each word."

I'll bet you are so proud of how well you read now. You read well enough to read some of the newspaper! Now you can become a better reader by reading a lot to your mother, brother, neighbors, or other friends. There are so many good books. You will be very busy!

pho to graph

poi son ing

rat tle snake

min er al

REVIEW
Reading Long Words

▶ "You read the parts, then read the word fast."

- -

department

amusement

ownership

collection

▶ "You read the words by first breaking them into parts."

(See the Additional Supplementary Reading Scope and Sequence in the *Tutor Handbook* for additional titles.)

Book Reading

▶ Read student's favorite stories!

Mastery Test 10

Use with Mastery Test 10—Tester Recording Sheet (see *Tutor Handbook*).

Sounds

► "Point to each letter or word part and say the sound."

–le	be–	de–
pre–	re–	ir
–tion	–sion	ur
ey	oi	oy
ow	ph	

· ·

(Provide student with Mastery Test 10—Student Recording Sheet found in *Tutor Handbook*.)

"Write the letters that make the _____ sound."

Word Reading

► "Sound these words out, then read them fast."

blow	alphabet	owner
loyal	spoiled	turkey
dribble	mission	action
prevent	repay	burst
began	detach	tickle
remote	beside	delight

(Provide student with Mastery Test 10—Student Recording Sheet found in *Tutor Handbook*.)

brother	should	busy	bought
sorry	beautiful	laugh	thought
wouldn't	mother	could	hold
piece	strange	cold	other
neighbor	through	eight	cookies
enough	lion	cherry	eggs
paper	toward	cried	tiny